CAMBRIDGE
UNIVERSITY PRESS

CAMBRIDGE ENGLISH
Language Assessment
Part of the University of Cambridge

Updated Second Edition

Kid's Box

Teacher's Resource Book 5

with Online Resources

American English

Kate Cory-Wright with Caroline Nixon
& Michael Tomlinson

Cambridge University Press
www.cambridge.org/elt

Cambridge English Language Assessment
www.cambridgeenglish.org

Information on this title: www.cambridge.org/9781316627389

First published 2009
Second edition 2015
Updated second edition 2017

Printed in Great Britain by CPI Group (UK) Ltd, Croydon CRO 4YY

A catalog record for this publication is available from the British Library

ISBN 978-1-316-62738-9 Teacher's Resource Book with Online Audio 5
ISBN 978-1-316-62755-6 Student's Book 5
ISBN 978-1-316-62721-1 Workbook with Online Resources 5
ISBN 978-1-316-62704-4 Teacher's Book 5
ISBN 978-1-316-62727-3 Class Audio CDs 5 (3 CDs)
ISBN 978-1-316-62791-4 Interactive DVD with Teacher's Booklet 5 (PAL/NTSC)
ISBN 978-1-316-62712-9 Presentation Plus 5
ISBN 978-1-316-63019-8 Posters 5

Additional resources for this publication at www.cambridge.org/elt/kidsboxamericanenglish

Thanks and acknowledgments

The authors would like to thank the following editors:

Bridget Kelly, Lynne Rushton and Liane Grainger

Kate Cory-Wright would also like to thank Janine Berger: freelance teacher trainer and materials writer, Quito, Ecuador.

The authors and publishers are grateful to the following illustrators:

FLP; Graham Kennedy; Gwyneth Williamson; Jo Taylor; Ken Oliver c/o The Art Agency; Lisa Smith c/o Sylvie Poggio; Theresa Tibbetts c/o Beehive

The authors and publishers are grateful to the following for permission to reproduce photographic material:

© jeff giniewicz / istock: p.21, © Graham Pearce / Shutterstock: p.35, © Vladimir Sazonov / istock: p.61, © Christian Musat / istock: p.61.

The publishers are grateful to the following contributors:

Pentacorbig: concept design, cover design, book design and page make-up
Wild Apple Design: second edition cover design and page make-up
John Green and Tim Woolf, TEFL Audio: audio recordings
Songs written and produced by Robert Lee, Dib Dib Dub Studios
hyphen S.A.: publishing management, American English edition

Contents

Introduction

- This Teacher's Resource Book is designed to help you and your students make the most of *Kid's Box 5,* as well as provide practice for the *Cambridge English: Young Learners* Tests. There are two main sections in this Book:
    - Worksheets
    - Practice tests

Worksheets

- There are two Reinforcement worksheets and two Extension worksheets per unit. The former are designed for review and to help those students who need extra practice, while the latter are designed to cater for the needs of fast finishers. These worksheets not only provide a resource for mixed-ability classes, but also offer material to set as homework or for the rest of the class to use while you work individually with a student on a Speaking test.
- Reinforcement worksheet 1 for each unit focuses on key structures, while Reinforcement worksheet 2 reviews vocabulary. Extension worksheet 1 is more challenging. It is designed for fast finishers who need a more cognitively demanding type of activity. Extension worksheet 2 is skills based. Reading, writing, listening, and speaking are practiced.
- There is also a Song worksheet for each unit. These always give the song lyrics and a song-based activity that varies from unit to unit. These worksheets are best done once students are familiar with the song. The songs are provided online on the *Kid's Box* website but you can also use the Class Audio CDs. Please note that the track numbers refer to *Kid's Box 5 Online Audio.*
- Finally, each unit has a content-based Topic worksheet. As explained in the Teacher's Edition, the content-based lessons in the Student's Book and Workbook aim to teach and reinforce understanding of subject topics that students learn in their other school classes, through the medium of English. Thus, there are dual aims: that of learning subject content and that of learning language. The Topic worksheets in this book add to the content-based pages in the Student's Book and Workbook.
- There is a page of teaching notes before the worksheets for each unit. These notes include Optional follow-up activities that add a useful extra dimension to each worksheet. You may find that one type of follow-up activity works better than another with your particular class, in which case you can use the suggestions as a springboard for adapting other worksheets.
- You may find, according to the particular interests of a student, that in one unit, he/she needs a Reinforcement worksheet while in other units, or at other times, the same student can more profitably do an Extension worksheet. Fast finishers may want/need to do Reinforcement and Extension worksheets.
- You can also use the worksheets as fillers or alternative activities when, for example, some other activity has interfered with the normal running of the class.
- The worksheets can also be used as models for you or your students to develop further practice activities. Creating exercises is an excellent way for students to consolidate their learning, and they will enjoy swapping them with their friends.
- You may find it useful to keep a record of the worksheets each student has completed.
- After the resources for each unit, there are two worksheets for each of the following festivals:
    - Christmas
    - Easter
- There are teaching notes for the Festivals section.

Practice tests

- There are four practice tests; the first covering the first three units of the Student's Book and the rest covering two units each. The tests are suitable for all classes, since they review the vocabulary and structures of the preceding units. In addition, they offer specific practice for the Flyers level of *Cambridge English: Young Learners* Tests. The focus here is on the various activity types and the test format.
- The more familiar the students are with these activity types, the more confidence they will have if they take Flyers, having completed *Kid's Box 6.*

Flyers activity types in *Kid's Box 5* tests

Task	Expected response	Tips
Listening 25 minutes		**Ensure students know that each listening text is heard twice.**

Task	Expected response	Tips
Part 1 Listening for names and descriptions	Draw lines to match names to people in a picture.	Familiarize students with the names in the tests and ensure that they know which names are male and female and which can be both: e.g., *Alex*, *Kim*, *Pat*, and *Sam*. Point out the example, where a line has been drawn from a name to a person in the picture. Students should listen to all the information about each person before making a decision. This information may be physical characteristics, clothes, actions, or locations. There may be two people with blond hair, but it will be other distinguishing features that identify exactly the person being spoken about.
Part 2 Listening for names, spellings, and other information	Write words or numbers.	Encourage students to look at the picture and the title and to understand the situation in which the information is being given. Get them to read the prompts and try to imagine the kind of answer, e.g., a day of the week, a time, a name, etc. Practice spelling out words for students to write down the letters correctly and saying large numbers up to 1001 and ordinals up to 31st.
Part 3 Listening for words, names, and detailed information	Match pictures with illustrated words or names by writing a letter in the box.	Students should read carefully the introductory question at the top of the page to help them understand the general content and context of the questions. Students should be aware that the information in the left-hand column is not given in the same order as on the recording. There are eight options given that the students have to match to the things in the left-hand column. They should be aware that, although all eight options are mentioned in the recording, only six of them are correct. They should not assume that the first word they hear is the correct one.
Part 4 Listening for specific information of various kinds	Check the box under the correct picture.	Ensure that students listen to the whole of each part of the dialog before deciding on their answer. All three picture options are mentioned, but only one is correct.
Part 5 Listening for words, colors, and specific information	Carry out instructions to color, and write.	Practice color vocabulary (*black*, *blue*, *brown*, *green*, *gray*, *orange*, *pink*, *purple*, *red*, *yellow*) and ensure that students have the necessary colored pencils for the test. There are two of each item in the picture. Teach students to listen carefully for the exact description and/or location to decide that item they have to color. Remind students that, as well as coloring, they have to write words on the picture.
Reading and Writing 40 minutes		**Correct spelling is required in all parts of the Reading and Writing Test.** Encourage students to write clearly. It is often better not to use cursive writing. Teach students to write only as much as they need to. Give time limits when doing classroom tasks, to help students learn time managment.
Part 1 Choosing the correct words to match given definitions	Copy correct words next to definitions.	Give students practice reading the whole sentence. There are often several possible options in the words around the text but only one that is completely correct. Discuss the different options with students and why only one of them is correct. Give students practice in accurate copying. Remind students to copy the whole option and not to add anything extra. Teach students to check and correct their spelling.

Task	Expected response	Tips
Part 2 Reading and completing a conversation by choosing the best response	Choose the correct response by writing a letter.	Remind students to read all the options before choosing the correct one. Remind them to take extra care not just to choose an answer because it has the same word in it as the statement before it. Point out that there are two answers that they do not need. Practice appropriate responses, not just to questions, but also to statements. Give practice with the use of set expressions, e.g., *Fine, thanks. / So do I,* and with short *yes/no* answers.
Part 3 Reading a story and choosing the best words to complete it	Choose and copy missing words correctly. Check a box to choose the best title for the story.	Encourage students to read the whole text before trying to complete the first blank and then to read the text immediately surrounding the blank. Give practice guessing which type of word (noun, adjective, singular, plural, verb, etc.) could go into a blank and then in choosing an appropriate word from the box. Give students practice reading stories and then giving a brief phrase to say what the gist of the story is.
Part 4 Reading and understanding a text and choosing grammatical words to complete it	Select the correct word from a choice of three options and copy it in the corresponding blank.	Encourage students to read the whole text before trying to complete the first blank, and then to read the text immediately surrounding the blank. They should then choose an appropriate word from the list. Remind students to choose a word only from the three options given and to copy it exactly into the space.
Part 5 Reading a story and completing sentences about the story	Complete sentences about a story by writing 1, 2, 3, or 4 words.	Remind students that there can be 1, 2, 3, or 4 words missing from each blank but that they should not write more than four words. Teach students to predict an outline of the story from the picture and the title. Give students practice in understanding what is being referred to in a text, especially the meaning of pronouns. All words in every answer are taken from the text. Students should ensure that words chosen to complete sentences are copied correctly.
Part 6 Reading a short text and providing the missing words	Complete a text by writing words in the blanks. No answer options given	Practice common collocations with students such as: *ask for, read about, take a photograph.* Encourage them to read the whole text and guess what words are missing. Remind them that there is only one word missing from each blank.
Part 7 Writing a story from 3 picture prompts	Write 20 or more words.	Encourage students to describe scenes. Review vocabulary in topic groups. Practice linking sentences.
Speaking 7–9 minutes		The Speaking tests are designed to test students' interactive listening ability, production of extended responses, and pronunciation. They are required to follow simple instructions, talk about different pictures, and to answer simple questions about themselves. If you can, arrange to swap classes with another English teaching co-worker, to give students the opportunity to work with someone that they may not know as well. Photocopy, color, and cut out the two "Find the Differences" scenes, the two "Find Information" cards, and the "Tell the Story" pictures. Mount them on cardboard, and laminate, if possible, for future use. Prepare Reinforcement or Extension worksheets for the rest of the class to do while you conduct the Speaking test with individual students. Make sure that each student feels comfortable before you begin the test. See the Test key and audioscript (pp 136 to 144) for instructions on how to begin each part of the four Speaking tests in this book.

Task	Expected response	Tips
Part 1 Understanding statements about a picture and responding with what is different about a second picture	Identify six differences between pictures.	The following examples are based on Units Welcome–2 Speaking test. Show the student both "Find the Differences" cards. Say that some things are different between the two pictures and give an example e.g., *In my picture, the teacher is wearing pants, but in your picture the teacher is wearing a skirt.* Then give the student his/her copy. Say: *I'm going to say something about my picture. You tell me how your picture is different.* Then describe your picture, without pointing at it, to elicit responses from the student. Teacher: *In my picture, two girls are talking*. Student: *In my picture, two girls are reading a book*. If necessary, point at the relevant difference, repeat your statement, and ask a back-up question: *What are the girls doing in your picture?* Give students practice in class in describing differences between two similar pictures. Ensure students can introduce themselves with their first name, last name, and age.
Part 2 Answering questions with short responses and asking questions to find out information	Ask and respond to questions about two people or objects or situations.	Briefly show the student both "Find Information" cards. Then give the student his/her copy. Introduce the subject and start to ask questions. The student should be able to answer the questions by looking at his/her card. Teacher: *This is Nick. I don't know anything about him but you do. So I'm going to ask you some questions. How old is Nick?* Student: *(He's) 13.* (T): *Does he think documentaries are interesting or boring?* (S): *Boring.* Help students by pointing at the relevant information if necessary. Complete the questions, then swap roles. Give students practice in class in asking and answering questions with question words *Who, What, When, Where, How old, How many,* etc. They should also be able to ask and answer questions with *or*, e.g., *Does he live in a house or an apartment?*
Part 3 Understanding the beginning of a story and then continuing it based on a series of pictures	Describe each picture in turn.	Show the student the "Tell the Story" card and give them time to look at it. Indicate the sequence by pointing. Introduce the story and describe the first picture: *These pictures tell a story. Just look at the pictures first. It's Tuesday. Michael is going to take a science test on Friday. He likes science and he wants to get a good mark. Now you go on telling the story.* Many variations in content and form are possible. If necessary, point at the pictures, and ask questions about them: *What time is it? What's Michael doing with his mom? Why? What's he going to do each day? What should/shouldn't he do when he is studying?* Do not expect long sentences or highly developed storytelling skills. Students should only be able to say a few words about each picture. Give students practice in class in telling picture stories.
Part 4 Understanding and responding to personal questions	Answer personal questions.	This part of the test is a chance for students to answer simple questions about themselves and their everyday lives that are related to the other parts of the test. The questions should cover a range of tenses that the students have already studied in class. For example, introduce the subject by asking about the student's evenings and continue asking questions to elicit responses. Teacher: *Now let's talk about your evenings. Are you going to watch TV tonight?* Student: *Yes.* (T): *What kind of TV shows do you like?* (S): *Cartoons.* (T): *What time do you go to bed?* (S): *(I go to bed) at nine o'clock.* Give students practice in class in answering questions about themselves, their families and friends, their homes, their school and free time activities, and their likes and dislikes. Make sure they know how to say: *Hello, Goodbye* and *Thank you* and *Sorry, I don't understand.*

Teacher's notes

Reinforcement worksheet 1

- Students guess which school subjects Sophia, Frank, and Oliver like / don't like. Then they read the texts and fill in the blanks. Students read the speech bubbles and decide which character said each one. Finally, students complete the last three speech bubbles based on their own interests and favorite subjects.

Key: 2) 1 Sophia likes music. She doesn't like history. 2 Frank likes science. He doesn't like computer studies. 3 Oliver likes art. He doesn't like geography. **3)** Oliver, Sophia, Frank.

- ***Optional follow-up activity:*** On four separate strips of paper, each student writes four sentences: two about what subjects they like and two about subjects they don't like. Students should use *like / don't like + ing*. Working in groups, they scramble the papers in the middle of the table, then take turns picking one up and reading it out. The group has to guess who wrote it.

Reinforcement worksheet 2

- Students look at the example words in the word search puzzle: *geography* and *P.E.* Point out that the words can go backward and upward, as well as forward and down. Students find the school subjects. They then complete the sentences with the words, by reading the definitions.

Key: 2) 2 dictionary, 3 P.E., 4 music, 5 geography, 6 art, 7 history, 8 Math, 9 exams, 10 French.

- ***Optional follow-up activity:*** Students work in groups miming subjects from the list for the others to guess.

Extension worksheet 1

- Check before using this worksheet that students can cope with the math and know the relevant symbols.
- Go through the example to establish that, in this case, a pattern is made by adding two each time. Students work out what they have to add for the other questions and then complete the patterns. Students do the math puzzles and write their answers in the crossword.

Key: 1) 1 eight, ten (increases by two each time), 2 twelve, fifteen (increases by three each time), 3 forty, fifty (increases by ten each time), 4 twenty-four, thirty (increases by six each time), 5 twenty-eight, thirty-five (increases by seven each time). **2)** 2 eleven, 3 fifteen, 4 twelve, 5 three, 6 twenty. The number across is **eleven**.

- ***Optional follow-up activity:*** Students write math puzzles for their friends. Encourage them to use words rather than figures.

Extension worksheet 2 F toward

- Remind students about the City School ezine. Students read the interview between the children and their principal and write in the correct questions from the list on the right. Then they listen to the interview to check their answers. They can practice the interview in groups of four.

Key: 2 Mr. Kelly: How can I help you? 3 Maria: How old is City School? 4 Dan: How many students are there? 5 Maria: When do children start school? 6 Dan: And when do children leave this school?

- ***Optional follow-up activity:*** Students prepare questions for a teacher in their school. Practice the questions with them. If possible, ask them to carry out their interview with a real teacher (or perform the interview in class with other students).

Song worksheet

- Students listen to the song and check subjects that the singers like. Point out some words in the first verse of the song with different numbers of syllables (e.g., *study*=2, *afternoon*=3). Ask students to clap the number of syllables. Then students circle the words as instructed in each verse. Now the class can sing the song.

Key: 1) Pictures checked should be: geography, history, science, P.E., languages. **2)** 1 because/Friday/study/morning, 2 I/and/to/too/my/in/the, 3 computer, 4 languages, Japanese, dictionary.

- ***Optional follow-up activity:*** Students play *Hangman* in class, using school subjects. When a student guesses the word, he/she says how many syllables the word has.

Topic worksheet

- Help students pronounce the word *archeologist* (*ar-kee-**ol**-o-gist*). Using the illustrations pre-teach: *skeleton, to dig, local, skull, tomb, cave,* and *gold.* Students read the text and label the remaining illustrations. Students then read the text again and correct the sentences.

Key: 1) staircase, King Tutankhamen, jewelry, archeologist. **2)** 2 Archeologists often find paintings in caves. 3 Teeth can tell archeologists how old the person was and what they ate. 4 The Incas lived in Machu Picchu more than five hundred years ago. 5 Howard Carter found King Tutankhamen after digging for six years / for a long time. 6 King Tutankhamen was found inside a big room / a tomb (behind a staircase and a wall).

- ***Optional follow-up activity:*** Students discuss and then write about the question: *Would you like to be an archeologist? Why? / Why not?*

Reinforcement worksheet 1

1 **Look at the pictures of Sophia, Frank, and Oliver. Guess their favorite school subjects. What subjects do you think they don't like?**

Sophia

Frank

Oliver

2 **Now read about them and complete the sentences. Were you right?**

Sophia	Frank	Oliver
I like singing and playing the guitar. I don't like learning about the past.	I like to learn about plants and the human body. I don't like the Internet.	I like taking photographs and drawing. I don't like learning about other countries.

1 Sophia likes ....music............ . She doesn't like ....

2 Frank likes .... He doesn't like ....

3 Oliver likes .... He doesn't like ....

3 **Who would like to put these things in the ezine? Write Sophia, Frank, or Oliver under the sentences.**

I'd like to put a painting in the ezine.

....

I'd like to write about my favorite singer and her new CD.

....

I'd like to write about animals and what they eat.

....

4 **Write three things that you would like to put in an ezine.**

I'd like to put .... in the ezine.

I'd like to write about ....

....

Reinforcement worksheet 2

1 Find and circle ten school subjects.

g	e	o	g	r	a	p	h	y
n	h	h	c	n	e	r	f	r
v	s	i	h	o	x	j	i	a
m	i	s	g	p	a	l	o	n
a	t	t	e	r	m	t	i	o
t	r	o	p	s	s	m	c	i
h	e	r	t	e	r	a	r	t
s	g	y	h	a	r	m	i	c
e	m	u	s	i	c	s	a	i
t	s	c	i	e	n	c	e	d

~~geography~~
~~P.E.~~
history
art
exams
dictionary
French
math
music
science

2 Complete the sentences using the school subjects.

1 I like science. We study animals, plants, and the human body in this subject.

2 I use a .... to help me understand new words.

3 Zee loves playing soccer and basketball. His favorite subject is ....

4 David likes .... He's good at singing, playing the guitar, and the piano.

5 We learn about different countries in ....

6 Sarah loves drawing and taking photographs. Her favorite subject is ....

7 In .... we can learn about the past.

8 Try this! 10 + 20 – 3 / 9 = 3. .... is easy!

9 We have to study a lot before we take ....

10 If you speak .... , you can talk to people in France.

Welcome!

Extension worksheet 1

1 Complete the number patterns. Write the numbers.

1

two	four	six	eight	ten

2

three	six	nine		

3

ten	twenty	thirty		

4

six	twelve	eighteen		

5

seven	fourteen	twenty-one		

2 Complete the math puzzles.
Write your answers in the crossword puzzle.
What's the number in the black boxes?

1 8 + 8 – 6 = ...10......

2 9 x 2 – 7 = ...

3 2 x 5 + 35 / 3 = ...

4 4 x 6 / 2 = ...

5 5 x 7 + 10 / 15 = ...

6 6 x 5 – 20 + 10 = ...

The number in the black boxes is:

....

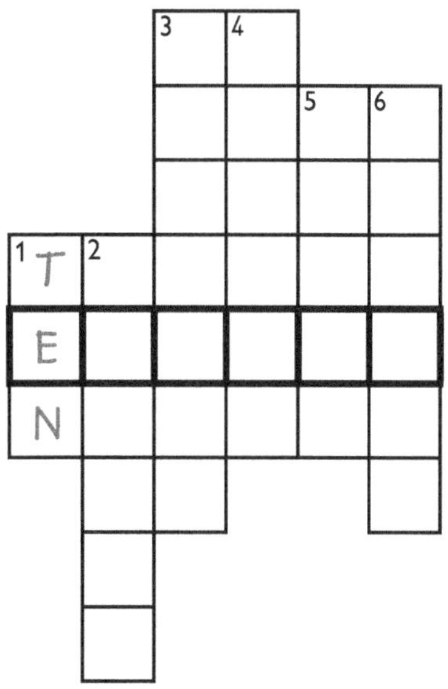

Welcome!

Extension worksheet 2

1 For their ezine, Alex, Maria, and Dan are interviewing Mr. Kelly, the principal of City School.

Read the questions and complete the interview.

Alex:	Good afternoon, Mr. Kelly.
	1 *How are you?*
Mr. Kelly:	I'm fine, thank you.
	2
Maria:	We'd like to ask you some questions for our ezine.
	3
Mr. Kelly:	It's fifty-seven years old.
Dan:	4
Mr. Kelly:	There are five hundred and eighty-three students.
Maria:	5
Mr. Kelly:	Children start school when they are four years old.
Dan:	6
Mr. Kelly:	When they're twelve.
Alex:	OK, that's all. Thank you!
Mr. Kelly:	You're welcome. Good luck with your ezine!

- How old is City School?
- When do children start school?
- ~~How are you?~~
- How many students are there?
- And when do children leave this school?
- How can I help you?

2 Listen and check.

Welcome!

Song worksheet

1 **3** **Listen and read. Check (✓) the pictures of the subjects that the singers like.**

 ✓

 ☐

 ☐

 ☐

 ☐

 ☐

☐

Because school is cool, it's where we go.
From Monday through Friday, I'm sure you know.
We study, and we play, that's what we do.
We do it in the morning and the afternoon!

I really love geography,
And I enjoy history,
I like to study science, too!
My favorite subject in the afternoon.

Before lunch we have music,
And then computer studies,
And on Wednesday we do sports.
That's a class that is too short!

And I like to do languages.
Spanish, French, and Japanese.
A lot of words in the dictionary,
For me to study and to read.

2

1 "Monday" has two syllables. Circle another two-syllable word in this verse.

2 Two one-syllable words are circled in this verse. Can you circle another one?

3 There is one three-syllable word in this verse. Can you circle it?

4 There are three three-syllable words in this verse. Can you circle them?

Welcome!

Topic worksheet

1 Read about archeologists. Label the pictures.

a cave

Archeologists are interested in history. They often travel to countries where people lived thousands of years ago. They look at paintings in caves and find bones. They find things that people used every day.

When archeologists find a skeleton, they ask many questions; for example, *How big is it? Is it a man, woman, or child? Why is it there?* Sometimes they find the person's skull. Teeth can tell us how old the person was and what they ate.

skeleton

to dig

Sometimes there are more questions than answers. Hiram Bingham went to Peru in South America. Local people told him about a "city" on a mountain. Bingham found "Machu Picchu." He learned a lot about the Incas who lived there more than five hundred years ago. But there are still many questions. *Why did the Incas live there? Why did they leave? Why were most of the skeletons women?*

A famous archeologist named Howard Carter dug in the sand in Egypt for six years. In 1922, he found a staircase and a wall. Behind these there was a big room. It was the tomb of King Tutankhamen. He was surrounded by jewelry and gold.

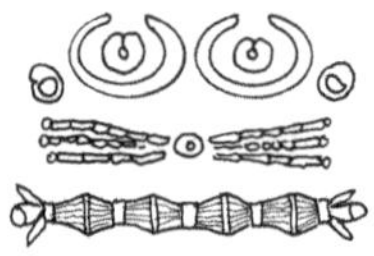

Archeologists work in the sun, the rain, and the cold. They look for answers for many years. Sometimes they never find them.

2 Correct the sentences.

1 Archeologists are interested in math.

Archeologists are interested in history.

2 Archeologists often find paintings in houses.

3 Teeth can tell archeologists the color of someone's hair.

4 The Incas live in Machu Picchu today.

5 Howard Carter found King Tutankhamen after digging for a short time.

6 King Tutankhamen was found on a mountain.

1 Teacher's notes

Reinforcement worksheet 1

- Students compare the schedules and write five more differences.

Key: 2 Crazy Cat / Cool Cat at 1:45, 3 School Friends Episode 5/3 at 2:15, 4 Golf/Soccer at 2:45, 5 The Rosetta Stone at 3:00/3:15, 6 Quiz / The Weather at 3:50.

- ***Optional follow-up activity:*** Students write a plan of their favorite TV schedule (real or imaginary). Display these in the classroom, and ask students to vote for their favorite.

Reinforcement worksheet 2

- Use the example to show students how to complete the missing word in each sentence, using the words on the TV, and then cross out each word as they use it. The aim is to cross four words in a straight line. The line can be horizontal or vertical, but not diagonal. Then use the first letter of these four words to complete Maria's sentence.

Key: 1) 2 channels, 3 quiz, 4 sports, 5 animals, 6 series, 7 boring, 8 weather, 9 turn on, 10 episodes. **2)** All the words in the last line on the right (***b****oring*, ***e****pisodes*, ***s****eries*, ***t****urn on*) are crossed out. Maria is saying *Shows about dinosaurs are the best*!

- ***Optional follow-up activity:*** Students invent definitions for the remaining six words: *cameraman, screen, action movie, music video, funny, cartoon.*

Extension worksheet 1

- Using a flashlight and a ball, explain that when the sun is in one half of the world, it's dark in the other half. Check students know the names of the cities and what countries they're in. Students then draw lines from the names to the dots on the map. Refer to an atlas if necessary. Then look at the map together, pointing out the different times in different places.

  Students write the time for each city using "in the morning/afternoon/at night." To help students with the number of hours' difference between the cities, look at the clocks and ask questions, e.g., *It's 11:15 in London. What time is it in Paris?* (12:15) *So how many hours ahead is Paris?* (1 hour) *If it's 8:00 in London, what time is it in Paris?* (9:00).

NY	**London**	Paris	Tokyo	Sydney
– 5	**0**	+ 1	+ 9	+ 11

  Choose different cities. Now students complete exercise 2.

Key: 2) 2 London: It's a quarter after eleven in the morning. 3 Paris: It's a quarter after twelve in the afternoon. 4 Tokyo: It's a quarter after eight at night. 5 Sydney: It's a quarter after ten at night. **3)** 1 It's a quarter after four in Paris. 2 It's ten after eight in London. 3 It's a quarter to eleven in Sydney. 4 It's Thursday in London!

- ***Optional follow-up activity:*** Play *Pelmanism*. Give each student four equally-sized pieces of thin cardboard. On two of the cards they draw a clock face with a time on it. On the other two they write the corresponding time for each clock in words. Check that the faces and times match for each pair of cards. Working in groups of four, students place their "clock" cards face down on one side of the table and the "words" cards face down on the other. The first student picks up a "clock face" card and says the time. If he/she is wrong, the card is replaced and the next student takes a turn. If he/she is correct, he/she can pick up a "words" card. If the two cards match, he/she keeps them. If not, he/she returns them to the table and the next student takes a turn. The student with the most pairs of cards at the end is the winner.

Extension worksheet 2

- Students read the TV Guide and write a word from the box for each channel. Then students read the guide a second time to help them circle the right answers to the questions.

Key: 1) Channel 2 – comedy, Channel 3 – series, Channel 4 – cartoon, Channel 5 – quiz. **2)** 2 a, 3 c, 4 b, 5 a.

- ***Optional follow-up activity:*** Students discuss which shows from the TV guide they would like to watch and why.

Song worksheet

- Students listen to and read the song and underline all the show words. Then they draw happy and sad faces in the circles next to the shows that the singer does/doesn't like. If necessary, help them with phrases like: *They're not for me / They're not my thing.*

Key: Happy faces – documentary, cartoon, sports, action movies. Sad faces – TV, the news and weather, TV.

- ***Optional follow-up activity:*** Students personalize the song by replacing the underlined words with other shows.

Topic worksheet

- Students discuss a TV series that they know and like, and who is involved in making it. Students read the text and match the jobs with the roles. Check their answers and help with any pronunciation difficulties.

Key: 2) 2 h, 3 b, 4 c, 5 e, 6 g, 7 f, 8 a.

- ***Optional follow-up activity:*** Review superlatives (e.g., *the biggest, the most beautiful*). Then ask students to discuss that movie-making job is the most interesting/important/difficult/fun. Students discuss which one they would like to do and why.

Unit 1

Reinforcement worksheet 1

Find six differences between Channel TV1 and TV2. Write your answers.

CHANNEL TV1	
1:00	The News
1:45	Crazy Cat cartoons
2:15	School Friends *Episode 5*
2:45	Golf
3:00	The Rosetta Stone
3:50	What do you know? (quiz show)

CHANNEL TV2	
1:30	The News
1:45	Cool Cat cartoons
2:15	School Friends *Episode 3*
2:45	Soccer
3:15	The Rosetta Stone
3:50	The Weather

1 On TV1 the news is on at one o'clock. On TV2 the news is on at half past one.

2 On TV1 Crazy Cat cartoons is on at a quarter to two. On TV2 is on at

3 ....

4 ....

5 ....

6 ....

Unit 1

Reinforcement worksheet 2

1 Complete the sentences and cross out the words on the TV.

1 The news __________ tells us what is happening in the world.

2 TV1 and TV2 are the names of two c__________ .

3 A TV competition where people answer questions is called a q__________ show.

4 We can watch soccer on a s__________ show.

5 Many cartoon characters are not people. They are a__________ .

6 A story that you watch each week is called a s__________ .

7 Some documentaries are not b__________ . They are interesting.

8 This show tells us if it is raining or snowing. It is called the w__________ .

9 You have to t__________ __________ the TV when you want to watch it.

10 The parts of a series that you watch each week are called e__________ .

channels	cameraman	screen	boring
quiz	action movie	sports	episodes
music video	weather	animals	series
funny	~~news~~	cartoon	turn on

2 Which four crossed out words form a line? Use the first letters to complete what Maria is saying.

Shows about dinosaurs are the __________!

Unit 1

Extension worksheet 1

1 Draw lines to each city.

New York, U.S.A. London, U.K. Paris, France Tokyo, Japan Sydney, Australia

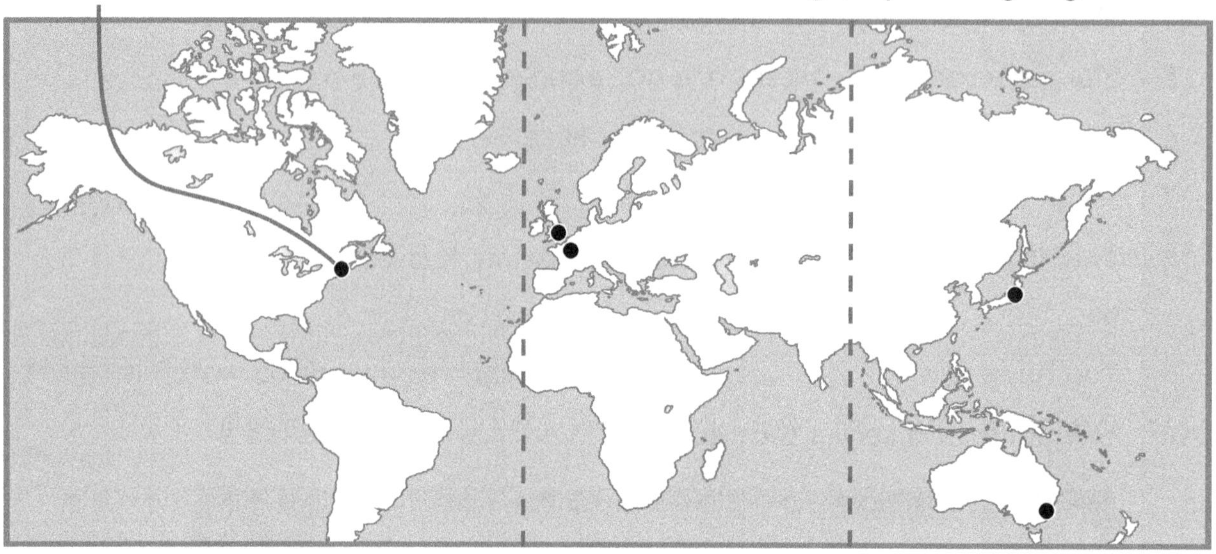

← MORNING →← AFTERNOON →← NIGHT →

2 Write the time in each city.

1 New York: It's a quarter after six in the morning.

2 London: ....

3 Paris: ....

4 Tokyo: ....

5 Sydney: ....

3 What time is it in these cities? Write your answers.

1 It's a quarter after three in London. What time is it in Paris?

It's a quarter after four in Paris.

2 It's ten after three in New York. What time is it in London?

It's ten after ....

3 It's a quarter to nine in Tokyo. What time is it in Sydney?

It's ....

4 It's twenty after seven on Friday morning in Sydney. What day is it in London?

....

Unit

Extension worksheet 2

1 Read the TV Guide and choose words from the box for each channel.

series	cartoon	~~documentary~~	the weather
quiz	music video	comedy	

Children's TV Guide

Channel 1	Channel 2	Channel 3	Channel 4	Channel 5
4:00–5:00 Dolphin and whale special	4:00–4:30 Clowntime	4:00–4:45 Happy street	4:00–5:40 Supermom 2	4:00–4:15 What do you know?
Do you know that dolphins never sleep? In today's show we learn all about these amazing animals: where they live, what they eat, and how smart they are.	Millie and Maisie the clowns are so funny! Why are they throwing paint and water? Why are they jumping up and down with eggs on their heads? Watch today's show to find the answers.	Last week Sam and Jane found an old map in the school library. Where did it come from? Where can it take them? This week's episode answers these questions and a lot more!	Now that Supermom's children are older, she's helping people with their animals! Did you lose your dog? Supermom can fly over the city and find it. She's fast and she's strong. The drawings in this movie are great!	This show is so exciting that you want it to be longer! Six people answer very difficult questions. The winner gets a vacation in Egypt.
documentary	____________	____________	____________	____________

2 Read again and choose the right answer.

1 How long is *Supermom 2*?

a) half an hour **b)** an hour and fifteen minutes **c)** an hour and forty minutes

2 What time does *Happy Street* finish?

a) at a quarter to five **b)** at a quarter after five **c)** at a quarter to four

3 Which of these things don't the clowns use?

a)  **b)**  **c)** 

4 Dolphins are: **a)** not smart **b)** always awake **c)** very big birds

5 In *What do you know?* the winner gets:

a)  **b)**  **c)** 

Unit 1

Song worksheet

4 Listen and read. Underline the TV shows. Does the singer like these TV shows? Draw a happy or sad face in the circles.

I don't like TV, I don't like it much,
But there are some shows that I sometimes watch.
On channel one at ten after three,
There's a really good documentary
About animals and where they live,
What they do and what they eat,
And on channel four at five to two,
They put on a great cartoon.
At one o'clock and then at seven,
They show the news and then the weather.
They're not my thing, they're not for me,
But I like the sports at half past three.
But what I like, what I love the best,
Are the action movies, more than the rest.
They're on at a quarter after four,
And at ten after seven, but I want more.

I don't like TV, I don't like it much,
But there are some shows that I sometimes watch.

Unit 1

Topic worksheet

1 What's your favorite TV series? Do you know how it's made?

A TV series is a story that we watch in many parts (or *episodes*). Sometimes we can watch one, two, or more episodes in one week. Usually a TV series starts with an idea. If a producer likes the idea, he/she talks to a screenwriter, who writes the story. Then the producer speaks to a director, who has to decide where to film the series and what happens in each scene. Next the producer has to find money to pay for the series. After the movie is made, the editors cut the film and join it together. Then the producer has to sell the series to TV channels around the world. And then we watch it!

Who else makes the TV series?

You can often see a list of people who made the series at the end of a TV show: the casting director, actors, camera crew, and designers. Who are these people and what do they do?

Every series needs a good technical team, for example, a camera crew (the people who film the series). The TV series also needs people to manage the sound, lighting, and special effects. A lot of artists and designers also help make the series. They have to prepare the make-up and clothes for the actors, or design the set.

Of course, a good TV series needs good actors! They play the people in the series. The casting director has to choose the actors. Famous actors are expensive, so the casting director can't always choose famous people for the series!

2 Match the person with the job.

1	The editor	**a**	films the series.
2	The screenwriter	**b**	finds the money for the series.
3	The producer	**c**	chooses the actors.
4	The casting director	**d**	cuts the film and joins it together.
5	The director	**e**	decides what happens in each scene.
6	Actors	**f**	prepare the make-up and clothes.
7	Designers	**g**	play the people in the series.
8	The camera crew	**h**	writes the story.

2 Teacher's notes

Reinforcement worksheet 1

- Look at the advertisement. If necessary pre-teach: *talent competition, to tell jokes, to joke.* Students read the dialog and fill in the blanks, using the appropriate form of *going to.* Then students label the characters. After checking the answers, ask comprehension questions, e.g., *Is Peter really going to eat hamburgers?* (no), *What is Peter going to do?* (tell jokes).

Key: 1) 2 What are your friends going to do? 3 Mary's / Mary is going to dance. 4 What's / What is he going to do? 5 He's / He is going to play the guitar. 6 I'm / I am going to eat. 7 What are you going to eat? 8 You're / You are not going to eat hamburgers! 9 I'm / I am not going to do that! 10 What are you really going to do? 11 I'm / I am going to tell jokes. **2)** Peter, Mary.

- ***Optional follow-up activity:*** In groups of three, students act out the dialog. Remind "Peter" to be a bit naughty, and "Mom" and "Dad" to be shocked.

Reinforcement worksheet 2

- Students unscramble the words. Then they label each picture.

Key: 1 firefighter, 2 dentist, 3 mechanic, 4 designer, 5 actor, 6 manager, 7 nurse, 8 pilot, 9 cook, 10 artist, 11 scientist, 12 reporter.

- ***Optional follow-up activity:*** Students write scrambled words for others to guess from one of the following themes: school subjects, kinds of TV shows, days of the week.

Extension worksheet 1

- Practice asking and answering *yes/no* questions by giving a confident student a job title e.g., *dentist* and getting the class to ask him/her questions to guess what it is. He/She can only answer *yes* or *no*. Pre-teach *uniform* and *office.* Students read the interviews and figure out which job each child is going to do.

Key: 2 basketball player, 3 mechanic, 4 pilot, 5 cook.

- ***Optional follow-up activity:*** Students interview each other in the same way, with *yes/no* questions to find out which job their partner has chosen.

Extension worksheet 2

- Students look at the picture and discuss the questions. Listen to student's thoughts. Students listen to the recording and complete the table. You may want to go through each character one by one, playing the recording several times.

Key (audioscript): John: I usually work *on the weekends* because that's when people have parties. I go to *people's houses* and wear a red nose. I use balls and do things to make people laugh. I love my job because *it's happy and it's fun!* (He's a clown.)

Robert: I work from *Monday to Friday* in *an office.* I make telephone calls and use a computer to type important letters and emails. I tell people what to do. I like this job because *I love working with people, and I'm never tired!* (He's a manager.)

Emma: I go to work *every night.* I work *in a busy hospital.* I'm not a doctor, but I help people who are sick or injured. I'm often tired but *my job is always interesting.* That's why I love it! (She's a nurse.)

Jane: I do my job *from half past seven in the morning to five in the afternoon.* I have to get up very early so that I can get to *school* before my students arrive. I work very hard teaching children to speak French. *It's really good to work with children.* I don't want to do anything else! (She's a French teacher.)

- ***Optional follow-up activity:*** Students imagine they do one of these jobs and write about their normal day at work for an ezine.

Song worksheet

- Students listen to the song and fill in the blanks. They then draw a picture in each box to represent an action for each verse.

Key: work, best, sleep x3, show, good, help, in x3, job, day, best, sleep.

- ***Optional follow-up activity:*** Ask the whole class to choose a job and make up a verse about it together. Students then choose a job for themselves and write their own verse. They can try to make it rhyme if they feel confident enough. The new verses could be written on the board and then sung by the class.

Topic worksheet

- Pre-teach: *earn* and *factories.* Students read the text and answer the questions. Finally, students draw a picture of a present they would like to give to a poor child, and write a short description of the present, and why they want to give it.

Key: 1) 1 They grow food in fields/on farms, they sell candy, they clean shoes, they make shoes and clothes in factories, they ask people for money in the streets. 2 Answers might include: beds, food, toys, time (to play), lessons, shoes, clothes, and candy.

- ***Optional follow-up activity:*** Write the following question and answers on the board and check that students understand them. Then put students in groups and ask them to rank the answers according to their importance and discuss. Question: *Why is education important?* Answers: *to learn to read and write, to find a good job, to meet friends, to know about the world, to have time to play and play sports, to learn languages, to learn about computers.*

Unit 2 Reinforcement worksheet 1

1 **Peter is talking to his mom and dad about the School Talent Competition. Complete what they say with *am/is/are going to.***

SCHOOL TALENT COMPETITION

Can you dance? Can you act? Are you good at singing or playing the guitar? Come to the Talent Competition! There are going to be a lot of prizes!

See you on Friday 24th at 8p.m.!

Mom: What (1) ...are... you ...going to... do in the School Talent Competition?

Peter: I don't know, Mom.

Dad: Well, what (2) .... your friends .... do?

Peter: Mary (3) .... dance. But I hate dancing.

Mom: What about John? What (4) .... he .... do?

Peter: He (5) .... play the guitar.

Dad: You're good at playing the guitar, Peter. Why don't you do that?

Peter: No, I don't like playing the guitar. Wait! I have a good idea.
I (6) .... eat!

Mom: Eat? What (7) .... you .... eat?

Peter: Five hamburgers in two minutes!

Dad: Oh, Peter! You (8) .... not .... eat hamburgers!

Mom: No, Peter. That's not a very good idea!

Peter: I'm joking. Of course I (9) .... not .... do that!

Mom: What (10) .... you really .... do?

Peter: I (11) .... tell jokes. I'm good at telling jokes!

2 **Write the names under the pictures.**

...John...

....

....

Unit 2

Reinforcement worksheet 2

Find the words and label the pictures.

eruns	nurse	sntedit	d....................
edsiengr	d....................	torca	a....................
steincsit	s....................	tereporr	r....................
chemanci	m....................	iltop	p....................
eieffigrhtr	f....................	okoc	c....................
mnaarge	m....................	ttiasr	a....................

1 ....

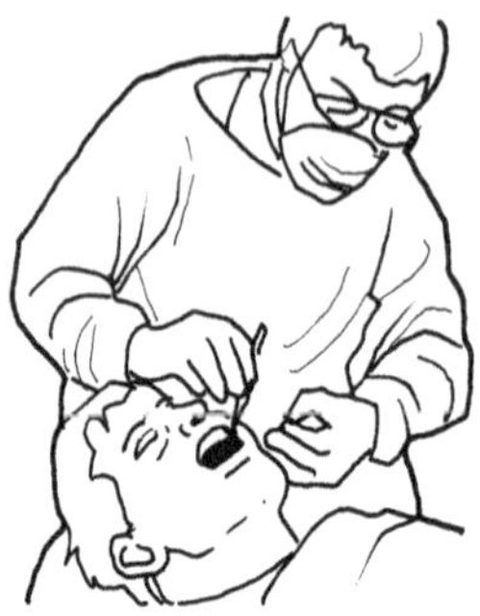

2 ....

3 ....

4 ....

5 ....

6 ....

7 nurse

8 ....

9 ....

10 ....

11 ....

12 ....

Unit 2 Extension worksheet 1

Students from City School are asking each other questions about what job they are going to do. They can only answer *yes* or *no*! Read their interviews and find the job.

painter	basketball player	pilot	soccer player
manager	mechanic	~~writer~~	cook

1

Are you going to work with other people?
In this job, are you going to use a laptop?
Are you going to work in an office?
Are you going to work at home?
Are you going to be a writer ?

No.
Yes.
No.
Yes.
Yes!

2

Are you going to work in the same place every day?
Are you going to play sports?
Are you going to use your feet to move a ball?
Are you going to be a ______________________ ?

No.
Yes.
No.
Yes!

3

Are you going to work in the same place every day?
Are you going to use a laptop?
Are you going to use your hands?
Are you going to work with cars?
Are you going to be a ______________________ ?

Yes.
No.
Yes.
Yes.
Yes!

4

Are you going to work in the same place every day?
Are you going to go to a lot of different countries?
Are you going to wear a special uniform?
Is playing sports important for this job?
Are you going to be a ______________________ ?

No.
Yes.
Yes.
No.
Yes!

5

Are you going to work with other people?
Are you going to use a laptop in this job?
Are you going to make something?
Are you going to make something that people need every day?
Are you going to be a ______________________ ?

Yes.
No.
Yes.
Yes.
Yes!

Unit 2

Extension worksheet 2

1 **Look at the picture. What does this man do? When and where does he work? Does he enjoy his job?**

2 5 **Listen to the people talk about their jobs. Complete the chart. What do you think each person does?**

Name	When do they work?	Where do they work?	Why do they like their job?	What do you think they do?
John	on the weekends			
Robert				
Emma				
Jane				

Unit 2

Song worksheet

6 Listen and complete the song. Draw something that happens in each verse.

He's going to do the job,
He's going to ....work.......... all day.
He's going to do his .... ,
Then .... and play,
.... and play,
.... and play.

She's going to .... the kids,
She's going to teach .... rules.
She's going to .... them all,
And work .... schools,
Work .... schools,
Work .... schools.

They're going to do the .... ,
They're going to work all .... ,
They're going to do their .... ,
Then .... and play.

Unit 2

Topic worksheet

1 Read about children who don't go to school and answer the questions.

Are there some days when you don't want to go to school? Many children around the world don't go to school. But they don't stay at home either. These children have to work.

Some children work in the fields or on farms. They help grow food for their families to eat. Some children work in the cities selling candy or cleaning shoes to get money for their families. Some children make shoes or clothes in factories. And some children walk down the streets asking people for money.

Life is hard for these children. They work because they are very poor. Sometimes they don't have food. Sometimes, they don't have a bed to sleep in. These children don't have toys to play with, and they don't have time to play. If they go to school, they can't earn money and if they don't earn money, they can't buy food to eat.

So next time you don't want to go to school, think of the millions of children who can't go to school.

1 What kinds of work do poor children do? Find examples in the text.

a They grow food in the fields. b ....

c .... d ....

2 Find four things in the text that money can buy for us.

....

2 You are going to give a working child a present. Draw a picture of your present and write a note to him or her.

I would like to give you this because ....

....

....

....

....

3 Teacher's notes

Reinforcement worksheet 1

- Ask students to look at the map. Point out key places, like the river and the streets. Tell them that they are on *The High Street*, near the *bus stop*. Using the map, students read each dialog and circle the correct word.

Key: 2 past, 3 right, 4 first, 5 third.

- ***Optional follow-up activity:*** Students practice giving directions to different places. They can use the map or the classroom. To turn your classroom into a "map," move tables and chairs to make "streets." Label some chairs with key places, e.g., *park, zoo.* A student stands at the board and asks for directions. Students tell him/her how to get to the place. The student "walks the route" around the classroom.

Reinforcement worksheet 2

- Students unscramble the letters to make words for things in the town, then put the correct word under each picture. Then they complete the clues to find the treasure.

Key: 1) (from left to right) supermarket, hospital, bank, train station, bus stop, cab, post office, theater, college, museum, castle, hotel, stadium, police station, restaurant, airport. **2)** 1 school, 2 bank, 3 post office, 4 theater, 5 hotel, 6 museum. The treasure is in the **castle**.

- ***Optional follow-up activity:*** Students write clues for each other like the ones in exercise 2, to guess different places in the town. Confident students could try to make their own "treasure hunt" as in the worksheet.

Extension worksheet 1

- Students complete the sentences 1 to 8 with the superlative. Then students read sentences a–h and match them to 1 to 8.

Key: 1) 3 largest, 4 smallest, 5 fastest, 6 most beautiful, 7 most interesting, 8 oldest. **2)** b 1, c 4, d 3, e 7, f 2, g 6, h 5.

- ***Optional follow-up activity:*** Students imagine the ugliest/biggest/smallest or most beautiful building in the world and write about it. They can draw a picture too and present this to each other in small groups.

Extension worksheet 2

- Students listen to the children's directions and use colors to draw their routes home from school. Then students write directions to Katy's house.

Key: 1) (audioscript): Sally (example black line): I leave school, turn left and go down Blue Street. I cross The High Street and Low Road and go straight ahead. I live across from the fire station in the second house on the left.
Ben (blue line): I go down Blue Street and turn left into The High Street. Then I turn right into Green Street. I live in a big building on the left.
Helen (red line): I go down Blue Street and turn left into The High Street. I take the second street on the right. It's called Red Street. I live on the corner of Red Street and Low Road, across from the movie theater.
Fred (green line): I walk down Blue Street and cross The High Street. I turn left into Low Road and then right at Green Street. I live across from the supermarket, the third house on the left.
Jim (brown line): I walk down Blue Street and turn left at The High Street. Then I take the first left and walk to the end of Green Street. I live in a boat on the River Eight.
2) Walk down Blue Street and turn left into The High Street. Then take the first right at Green Street. I live next to the Bookstore. (Other routes are possible.)

- ***Optional follow-up activity:*** Students write directions from their school to their homes. If they live too far away, they can give directions to places closer to the school.

Song worksheet

- Students match the rhyming words and add them to the words of the song. Play the song to check their answers. Ask students to skim read the song, looking for places (e.g., *theater*) and check the pictures of places in the list that the singer visited to find the five places he didn't visit. Now they sing the song.

Key: 1) 2 d, 3 a, 4 e, 5 b. **2)** See Student's Book, page 31. **4)** He *didn't* visit the toy store, bank, swimming pool, library.

- ***Optional follow-up activity:*** Draw two columns on the board. Label them *street/eat* and *late/eight.* Point out the different spelling of similar sounds. In small groups students think of more words that rhyme with *street/eat* and *late/eight.* They write them on the board. They earn points for each correct word. (Ideas: *street/eat – feet, meat, seat, cheat, meet; late/eight – date, plate, ate.*)

Topic worksheet

- Ask students if they can think of a castle in a movie or cartoon. Can they describe it and say who lives there? Pre-teach: *king, enemies, soldiers, holes, arrows, boiling oil, play tricks on.* Students read the text and underline three things they find interesting. They can use the labeled photograph to help them with vocabulary. Students then look at the words for parts of a castle. In class students talk about what they know about the parts of a castle and what they found interesting.

- ***Optional follow-up activity:*** Students draw and label a "fantasy" castle they would like to live in. How is the castle protected from enemies? Students show and describe their castles to the class or display them on the walls.

Reinforcement worksheet 1

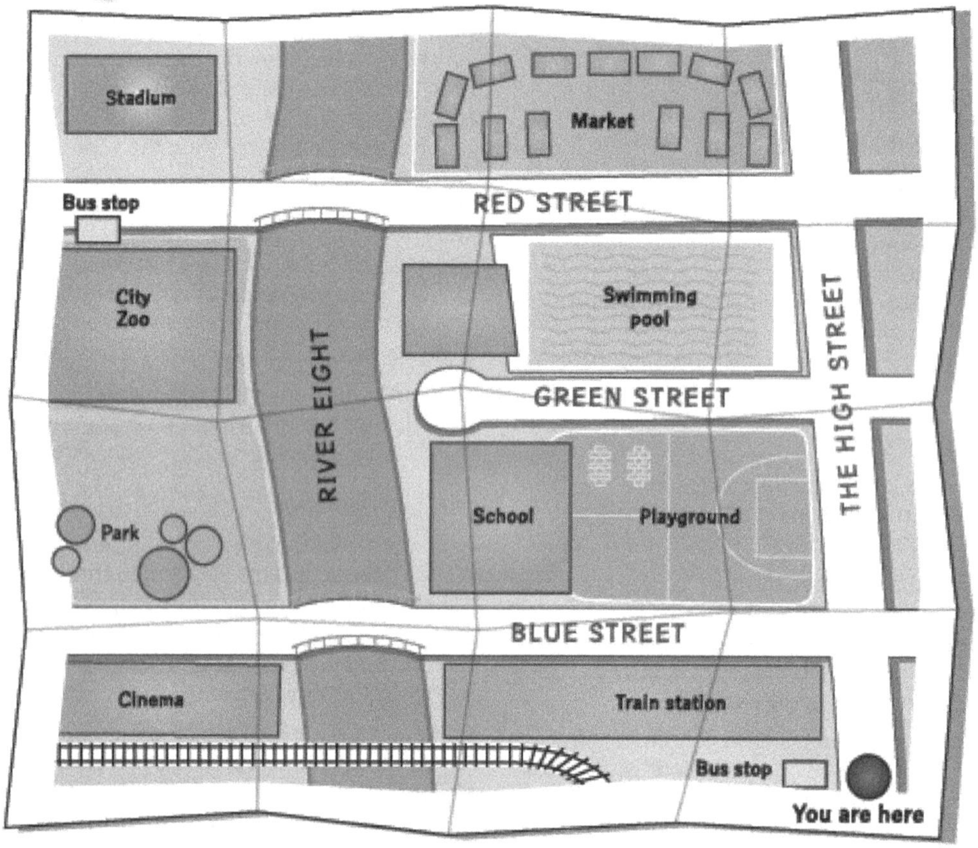

Find *You are here* on the map. Circle the correct words.

1 *Excuse me. Where's the playground?*

Go straight ahead and turn into Blue Street. The playground is on the corner. It's across from / next to the train station.

2 *Excuse me. Where's the park?*

Go down the High Street. Take the first street on the left. Walk across / past the school. Cross the bridge and the park is on the right.

3 *Excuse me. Where's the swimming pool?*

Go down the High Street and turn left into Green Street. The swimming pool's on the right / left.

4 *Excuse me. Can you help me? Where's the movie theater?*

Go straight ahead and take the first / second street on the left. Walk past the train station and across the bridge. It's on the left.

5 *Excuse me. Can you help me? I'm looking for the zoo.*

Go down the High Street. Take the second / third street on the left. Go past the swimming pool. Cross the river. It's on the left.

Unit 3

Reinforcement worksheet 2

1 Find the words and label the pictures.

sbu tops	bus stop	letho	______
retrasuant	______	iraropt	______
acb	______	tereath	______
tasidum	______	stop cffioe	______
egcleol	______	uumems	______
csalet	______	ocelpi atstino	______

2 Some treasure is hidden in one of these places. Complete the answers to the clues to find out where it is!

1 People come here to learn. s [c] h o o l

2 We visit the _ [ ] _ _ to get money.

3 We go to the _ _ [ ] _ _ _ _ _ _ _ _ to buy stamps.

4 We go to the [ ] _ _ _ _ _ _ _ to watch plays.

5 When we are not at home, we often sleep in a _ _ _ _ [ ].

6 We go to a _ _ _ [ ] _ _ to look at old things that tell us about history.

The treasure is in the c _ _ _ _ _ **!**

Unit 3

Extension worksheet 1

1 Use the words in parentheses to complete the sentences.

1 The world's biggest (big) train station is The Grand Central Terminal in New York, U.S.A.

2 The most expensive (expensive) cab ride in the world was a trip from London to Africa!

3 The .... (large) palace in the world is owned by a very rich man, the Sultan of Brunei.

4 The world's .... (small) museum is in the U.S.A.

5 The .... (fast) flight across the Atlantic Ocean took 1 hour, 54 minutes, 56.4 seconds.

6 One of the .... (beautiful) castles in the world is in Prague.

7 The world's .... (interesting) hotel is the Ice Hotel in Sweden. It's very cold inside!

8 The .... (old) stamp is called a Penny Black.

2 Find more information about sentences 1–8.

a People first used it on their letters in 1840. 8

b More than 550 trains use it every day. ....

c It has only one room! ....

d His home has 1,778 rooms and 257 bathrooms. ....

e It has an ice theater and an ice church. ....

f The passenger paid 62,908 U.S. dollars! ....

g It is also the biggest castle in the world. ....

h The pilots flew from New York to London. ....

Extension worksheet 2

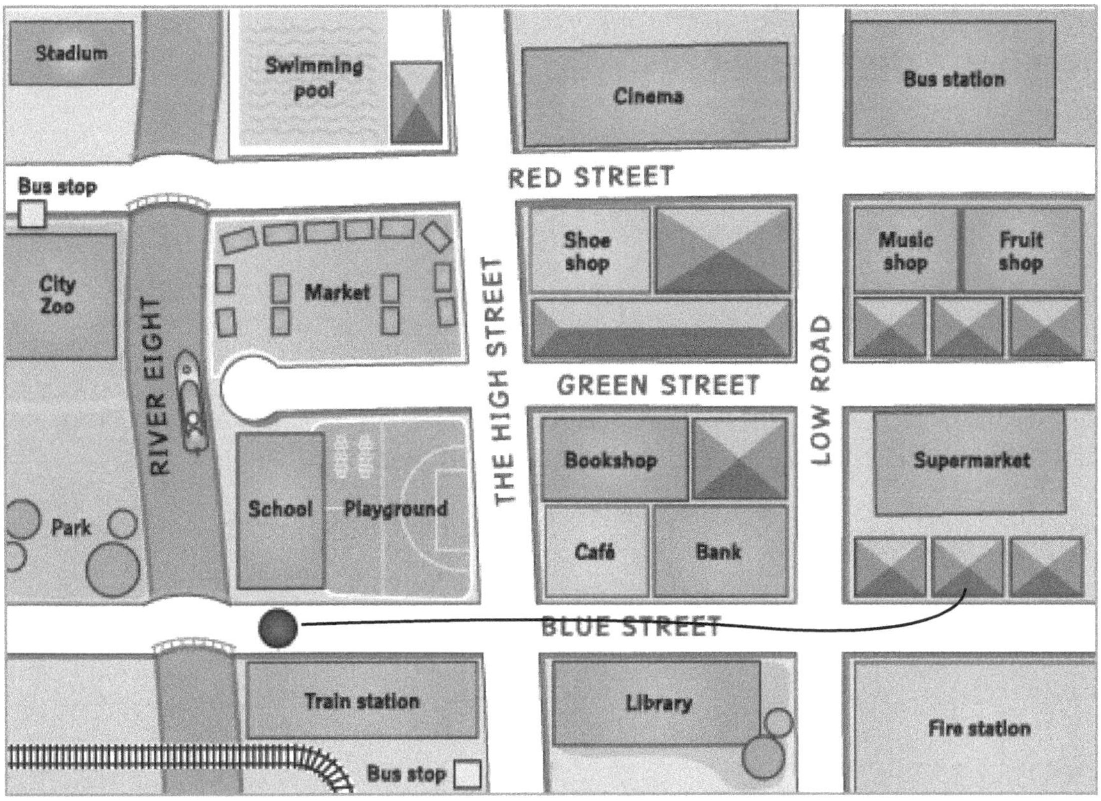

1 **7** **Look at the map and listen to Sally. She is talking about how she gets home from school. Then listen to the other children. Draw how they get home in these colors. The first one has been done for you.**

Sally	➜	black	Fred	➜	green
Ben	➜	blue	Jim	➜	brown
Helen	➜	red			

2

Katy

Unit 3

Song worksheet

1 Match the rhyming words.

1	hotel	a	too
2	day	b	eight
3	zoo	c	tell
4	street	d	play
5	late	e	eat

2 Complete the song with the rhyming words.

Theater, movies,
Restaurant and hotel,
Museum, castle,
A story to ___tell___ .

I went to London,
To have a nice day.
To go to a museum and
The theater for a ______________ .

I saw Tower Bridge,
And the castle, ______________ .
Walked in the park,
And went to the zoo.

I went to a restaurant,
On the corner of the street.
I sat outside and
I had something to ______________ .

I took a taxi,
Because it was ______________ .
My train was in the station.
It was half past eight.

Theater, movies,
Restaurant and ______________ ,
Museum, castle,
A story to tell.

3 8 Listen and check your answers. Then sing the song.

4 Look and check (✓) the places he visited. Which places *didn't* he visit?

Unit 3

Topic worksheet

1 Read about castles. Underline three interesting facts.

Hundreds of years ago, kings built castles to keep out their enemies. Sometimes thousands of soldiers lived inside the castle, usually in the **towers**. The king and his family usually lived in the **keep**.

Castles were strong. The walls were very thick and there were strong gates and a **portcullis** at the door. It was difficult for the enemy to break the gates and walls.

Castles were often on a hill. Why? First, it was difficult for enemies to climb the hill. Second, it was easy for the soldiers in the castle to see their enemies from far away. Many castles had water (**a moat**) around them.

A castle with a moat also had a **drawbridge**. If the enemy came close to the castle, the soldiers closed the drawbridge. Then their enemies could not cross the moat. Many people fell into the water. Then the soldiers sent arrows at the enemies from small holes in the towers (**arrow slits**).

If the enemies came into the castle, the soldiers played horrible tricks on them. For example, some castles had special floors that broke when the enemies came up the stairs. Castles also had **murder holes** (holes in the ceiling inside the keep). Soldiers waited at these places and threw boiling oil on their enemies.

2 What do you know about these parts of a castle?

towers, moat, drawbridge, keep, arrow slits, portcullis, murder holes

4 Teacher's notes

Reinforcement worksheet 1

- Students fill in the sentences with *was/were* and the simple past of the verb in parentheses. They then match the sentences to the pictures. Finally they draw a picture of something that happened to them and write a sentence about it using the simple past and past progressive.

Key: 1) 2 were/arrived, 3 was/hurt, 4 was/started, 5 were/saw, 6 was/dropped, 7 were/came. **2)** (clockwise from example) 1, 5, 2, 7, 6, 4, 3.

- ***Optional follow-up activity:*** Students act out one of the sentences. The class guesses the sentence. Help with any necessary corrections in use of tenses.

Reinforcement worksheet 2

- If necessary, review ordinal numbers. Students answer the questions about the times of the year. Then students figure out the "disaster" words based on the positions of the letters in the alphabet and the clues.

Key: 1) 2 August, 3 October, 4 December, 5 July, 6 April, 7 summer, 8 fall. **2)** 2 earthquake, 3 storm, 4 iceberg, 5 tsunami, 6 volcano.

- ***Optional follow-up activity:*** Students write similar clues for their classmates to test months of the year, "disaster" words and ordinal numbers.

Extension worksheet 1

- Students use the pictures to choose the correct words for each sentence. Model the first one with students and then let them continue on their own. Finally, students copy out the sentences paying attention to spelling and punctuation.

Key: I was giving the bird some food when a mouse ran past. The cat was running after the mouse when the dog woke up. The dog was jumping on the cat when it hit me. We were going to the hospital, when I remembered that the bird was still hungry!

- ***Optional follow-up activity:*** Students prepare their own sentence mazes for each other to practice past progressive and simple past.

Extension worksheet 2

- Cut the photocopied worksheet in half. Elicit/Pre-teach: *tsunami, volcano, ocean, steam, magma, rocks, fire, erupt.* Explain that the *Code* system helps scientists to know about these disasters before they happen and how dangerous they are going to be. The different color codes mean different levels of danger. Students work in pairs for this information exchange activity. Student A begins. He/She tells his/her partner about the three warning stages of a tsunami. Student B listens and draws pictures to illustrate what happens in the appropriate boxes. Then Student B tells her/his partner about each of the warning stages of a volcano while Student A draws.
- ***Optional follow-up activity:*** Students imagine that they are reporters and write news reports about an erupting volcano or an imminent tsunami. They can use the information on the worksheet to explain what scientists did/are doing and what is happening/going to happen.

Song worksheet

- Students read through the song once before you do actions for different lines of the song. Students shout out the line number. Then students listen to the song and cross out the extra word in each line.

Key: See Student's Book, page 37. The extra words are: 2 quickly, 3 heavy, 4 big, 5 slowly, 6 beautiful, 7 soccer, 8 chocolate, 9 all, 10 blue, 11 stone, 12 tall.

- ***Optional follow-up activity:*** Students play a Pictionary-style game in teams of two against two plus one judge. Each team writes four sentences using the past progressive and simple past, e.g., *I was swimming in a river when I saw a bear.* The two teams swap the sentences they have written. One student from each team picks a sentence and draws the meaning for their partner to guess the sentence. Then they swap roles and pick another sentence. The pair who guess all four sentences the quickest wins. The judge is there to time the pairs, to make sure no one cheats and to say who wins.

Topic worksheet

- Introduce the topic by asking if students know any stories about floods, e.g., *Noah's Ark*. Explain that they are going to read four famous "flood" stories (if possible, bring a map of the world so that you can show them where the stories come from). Pre-teach: *destroy, survive, greedy.* Students read the stories and label the pictures 1–4. As a class, discuss the question at the end of the text.

Key: The order of the pictures is as follows: a 2, b 1, c 4, d 3.

- ***Optional follow-up activity:*** Tell your students a very old/traditional story that you know. Then ask them if they can tell you one.

Unit 4

Reinforcement worksheet 1

1 **Complete the sentences with *was* or *were* and the past of the word in parentheses.**

1

1 I ....was.... sailing in my boat when the storm ....began.... (begin).

2 You .... talking to your friends when the cab .... (arrive).

3 Bill .... walking down the mountain when he .... (hurt) his leg.

4 I .... acting in a play when I .... (start) to cough.

5 They .... swimming in the ocean when the shark .... (see) them.

6 Maria .... talking to her mother when she .... (drop) her cell phone.

7 We .... having a picnic lunch when the rain .... (come).

2 **Write the numbers of the sentences next to the pictures.**

3 **Draw a picture and write a sentence about something that happened to you. Use *was/were + ing* and the past.**

Unit 4

Reinforcement worksheet 2

1 Answer the questions.

1 What's the third month after February? May

2 What's the second month after June? ____________

3 What's the seventh month after March? ____________

4 What's the month before January? ____________

5 What's the tenth month after September? ____________

6 What's the fifth month after November? ____________

7 What's the season after spring? ____________

8 What's the season before winter? ____________

2 Read the clues and use the code to write the disaster words.

1 This word begins with the eighth letter of the alphabet. It's a very strong and dangerous wind. h u r r i c a n e

2 This disaster happens when the earth moves. It begins and ends with the fifth letter of the alphabet. _ _ _ _ _ _ _ _ _ _

3 This weather word begins with the nineteenth, twentieth, and fifteenth letters of the alphabet. _ _ _ _ _

4 When it was sailing across the Atlantic Ocean in 1912, the Titanic hit one of these. It ends with the seventh letter of the alphabet. It was an _ _ _ _ _ _ _ _.

5 This word begins with the twentieth and nineteenth letters of the alphabet. It means a very big wall of ocean water. _ _ _ _ _ _ _

6 This word begins with the twenty-second letter of the alphabet and ends with the fifteenth. It's a disaster when one of these erupts! _ _ _ _ _ _ _

Unit 4

Extension worksheet 1

1 Look at the pictures and join the correct words in the sentences.

 I	gave	the bird	some food	when	a bird	ran	past.
	was giving	the mouse	some milk		a mouse	was running	
	give	the cat	some help		a bat	runs	

 The cat	was running after	the bird	when	the dog	woke	up.
	ran after	the mouse		the cat	wakes	
	runs after	the cat		the mouse	is waking	

 The dog	jumped on	the mouse	when	it hit	me.
	jumps on	the cat		it was hitting	
	was jumping on	the dog		it hits	

 We	went	to the farm	when	I remembered that	the dog	was still	hungry!
	go	to the hospital		I remember that	the bird	is still	
	were going	to the movie theater		I am remembering that	the cat	is still being	

2 Copy the sentences from the story. Be careful with your spelling!

Unit 4

Extension worksheet 2

Student A – Tell your partner about the warning stages of a *tsunami.* Then listen to your partner tell you about the warning stages of a *volcano* and draw pictures of them in the code yellow, orange, and red boxes.

TSUNAMI	CODE YELLOW watch carefully	CODE ORANGE very dangerous	CODE RED disaster!
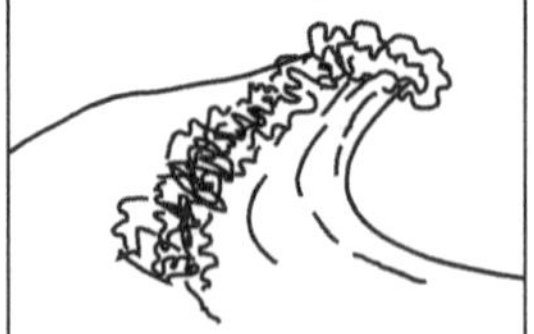	A tsunami is possible. Scientists are looking at their computers.	There is an earthquake under the ocean. There is going to be a tsunami in 6–9 hours.	People who live close to the ocean have to leave their homes. Soon there is going to be a very big wave.

VOLCANO	CODE YELLOW watch carefully	CODE ORANGE very dangerous	CODE RED disaster!
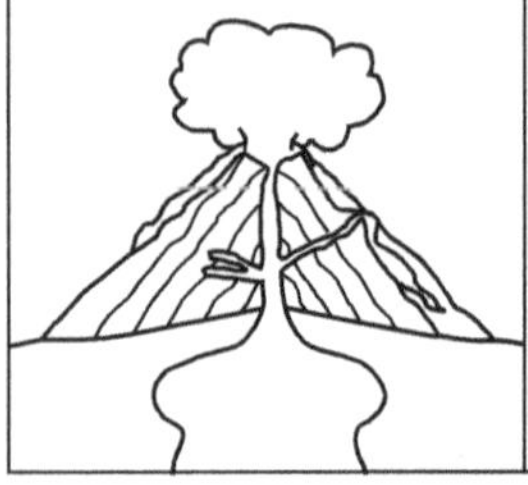			

Student B – Listen to your partner tell you about the warning stages of a *tsunami* and draw pictures of them in the code yellow, orange, and red boxes. Then tell your partner about the warning stages of a *volcano.*

TSUNAMI	CODE YELLOW watch carefully	CODE ORANGE very dangerous	CODE RED disaster!
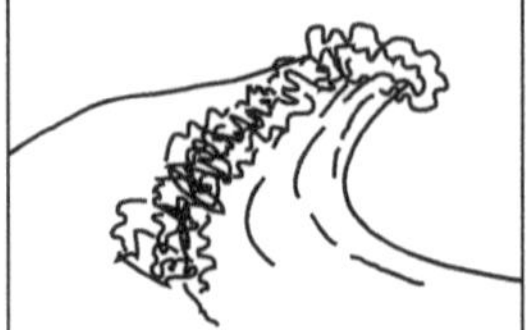			

VOLCANO	CODE YELLOW watch carefully	CODE ORANGE very dangerous	CODE RED disaster!
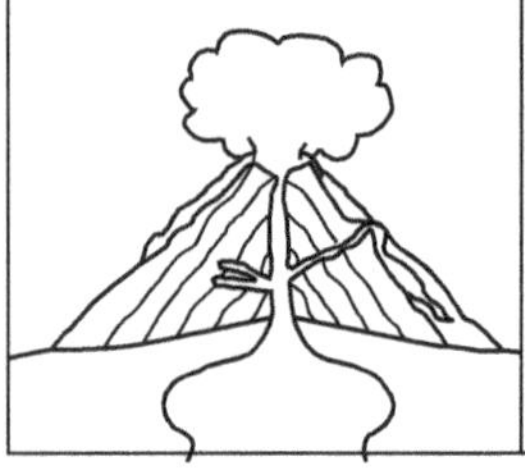	Scientists can see on their computers that the volcano is starting to move. There is steam coming out of the top.	The volcano is beginning to erupt. Magma is starting to come out of the top.	The volcano is erupting. It's very dangerous. It is throwing rocks and fire out of the top. People have to leave their homes.

Unit 4

Song worksheet

1 Read the song. Which line is your teacher acting?

2 9 Listen and cross out the extra word in each line.

1 What were you doing when the ~~crazy~~ storm began?

2 When the lightning hit and the water ran quickly.

3 Where were you when the heavy rain came down?

4 On the mountain, at the beach, in the forest, or the big town.

5 I was walking slowly up the mountain,

6 He was skating over the beautiful lake,

7 We were playing soccer in the park,

8 She was eating a piece of chocolate cake.

9 They were all swimming in the river,

10 He was sailing on the blue ocean,

11 She was climbing up a stone wall,

12 I was sitting under a tall tree.

Unit 4

Topic worksheet

1 In many countries there are stories about a lot of rain and a big flood that destroyed almost everyone on earth. Read the stories and label the pictures 1–4.

a

b

c

d

1 **Ivory Coast, Africa**
A good, kind man gave everything he had to the animals. Then he gave his last meal to the god Ouende. Ouende thanked the good man and told him to leave his home. Then Ouende sent six months of rain to destroy all the bad people. Today all the people of the world are from the family of the good man.

3 **Siberia, Asia**
The rain didn't stop for seven days. Some people and animals survived the flood because they climbed trees. Other people moved to different places. This is why people speak different languages today.

2 **Philippines, Asia**
Water covered the whole earth. Only two men and a woman survived. They went to the ocean. A great bird carried them on its back to their new homes.

4 **Guyana, South America**
Soon after people arrived on earth, all food grew on one tree. Makunaima and his four brothers cut down the tree. Water poured from the tree and there were a lot of fish in the water. One of the brothers tried to stop the water because he was worried about a flood. But Makunaima was greedy and he wanted more fish. So the water flooded the earth.

2 If people in different countries tell this story, do you think there was a big flood? What parts of the stories do you think are true?

5 Teacher's notes

Reinforcement worksheet 1

- Pre-teach: *cocoa beans, jungle, smell, cotton*. Students read the advertisement and complete the blanks with the *made of* structures provided. Then they unscramble and answer the questions. Students talk about question 3.

Key: 1) 2 is not / isn't made of, 3 is made of, 4 are made of, 5 are not / aren't made of, 6 are made of. **2)** 1 What is the river made of? (chocolate) 2 What can you do in the afternoon? (go to Chocolate School) 3 What is chocolate made from? (cocoa beans).

- ***Optional follow-up activity:*** Students work in groups and write a similar advertisement for a Museum of Candy.

Reinforcement worksheet 2

- Look at the examples. Point out to students that we don't use *- s* on the end of adjectives, even with plural nouns. Students make noun phrases from the nouns and adjectives and number the pictures. They then read the description to find the *What is it?* object, using the alphabet number code.

Key: 1) 3 a plastic toy, 4 metal keys, 5 a silver ring, 6 a cardboard box, 7 glass bottles, 8 a gold crown, 9 wool sweaters. **2)** (From left to right) 4, 1, 9, 2, 7, 8. **3)** The object is **a wooden table**. Point out *wooden* not *wood*.

- ***Optional follow-up activity:*** In pairs, students give clues about the objects in the list, e.g., where you put it/what you put in it/what you do with it/where you find it. Their partner guesses what the object is.

Extension worksheet 1

- Students figure out the missing word in each sentence and cross them out on the wall. Then they find three things that can be made with each of the four crossed out materials.

Key: 1) 2 wool 3 paper, 4 wood, 5 nylon, 6 hair, 7 metal, 8 stone, 9 sand, 10 fur, 11 plastic. **2)** The line of crossed out words is: paper, wool, plastic, nylon.

- ***Optional follow-up activity:*** Students list which things are natural and which things we make. (Natural: *oil, wood, hair, stone, sand, fur, rubber, bone, wool*. Things we make: *glass, metal, paper, nylon, plastic, sugar, chocolate*.)

Extension worksheet 2 F toward

- Students listen to the instructions , then color and write. They need the following three colors: green, red, yellow.

Key: 1 green box containing comic books, 2 PAPER written on left hand recycling bin, 3 yellow car closest to street corner, 4 red door next to man, 5 PLASTIC written on middle bin

Audioscript. FCH: Look at this picture of my family.
M: That's good, Daisy. What are they doing?
FCH: They're at the new recycling bins. My mom and my brothers are putting things in them.
M: This picture's in black and white. Do you want to color it?
FCH: OK. I can color my brother Nick's T-shirt.
M: Which boy is he?
FCH: He's putting a bottle into the bin on the right.
M: OK. Why don't you color his T-shirt black?

Can you see the black T-shirt? This is an example.

Now you listen and color and write.

1 M: Can you recycle a lot of different things there?
FCH: Yes, my mom's holding a lot of things in her box.
M: And there's a box full of paper on the ground.
FCH: Our old comic books are in that box. We have a lot!
M: You could color that box green.
FCH: OK.
2 M: There's no writing on the big recycling bins.
FCH: I know. Should I write on one of them?
M: You could write PAPER on that one on the left.
FCH: That's a good idea. I'm doing that now.
3 M: Your family has a lot of things to recycle.
FCH: Yes. And they're very heavy, too. We took them to the recycling bins in the car.
M: Is your car in the picture?
FCH: Yes. It's the one closest to the corner. It's yellow. I love it.
M: Well, I think you should color your car, too.
4 M: Who's that man? Is that your dad?
FCH: No, it's my friend May's dad. He's standing by their front door. Should I color the door?
M: OK. What color is their door?
FCH: It's red.
M: That's a nice color. Yes, do that.
5 FCH: Can I write something else now?
M: Yes, of course. Can you see the recycling bin in the middle?
FCH: Yes, I can. What's that for?
M: It's for plastic. Write that on the bin.
FCH: OK… I've done that now!
M: Good job! That's a very nice picture of your family, Daisy.

- ***Optional follow-up activity:*** Students ask each other questions about the picture, e.g., *Where are the people? What are the houses made of?* or describe things for the others to guess, e.g., *The small boy has it in his hand.*

Song worksheet

- Students listen to the song and find materials + objects as in the example. Students then choose any three objects from the song, draw pictures, and label them.

Key: a glass bowl, a wooden table, a grass skirt, a silver box, a gold watch, a wool scarf, paper books/cardboard book covers.

- ***Optional follow-up activity:*** Write four columns on the board headed *metal, glass, wood, silver*. Elicit things made of each material and make lists on the board. Students replace the objects in the song. For example, instead of *This chair is made of metal*, they can write *This box is made of metal*.

Topic worksheet

- Ask students to look at the picture of the landfill. What do they imagine is in there? Pre-teach: *garbage, landfill, throw away, decompose, hot dogs, underground, crazy*. Students read the article and underline three interesting facts and discuss. Then students list ten things they and their family threw away this week.
- ***Optional follow-up activity:*** Students draw a landfill with the things that they throw away and label the objects inside it. In groups, they discuss their ideas for recycling them instead.

Unit **5**

Reinforcement worksheet 1

1 Read about the Museum of Chocolate! Complete the sentences with *is made of* / *isn't made of* / *are made of* / *aren't made of.*

Museum of Chocolate

Do you like chocolate? Would you like to learn how chocolate is made? Come to the Museum of Chocolate!

You can see our museum by boat! You travel down the river and learn how chocolate is made. We have good boats, but don't fall in the river. The river (1) __is made of__ chocolate!

Don't miss Chocolate School in the afternoon. If you like art, you can learn how to paint and write with chocolate! If you prefer geography, explore our jungle to find cocoa beans. Chocolate is made from cocoa beans. The jungle (2) ____________ chocolate, but it smells beautiful!

Finally, don't forget to visit the Choc-Store! Buy a present that (3) ____________ chocolate. Our toys, pictures, and books (4) ____________ chocolate! But some presents in the Choc-Store (5) ____________ chocolate. The T-shirts, for example, (6) ____________ cotton!

2 Write the questions. Then answer them.

1 What / made / of / river / is / the / ?

____

2 can / do / you / afternoon / the / in / ? / What

____

3 chocolate / from / made / is / What / ?

____

3 Which "Chocolate School" class would you like to go to? Why?

Unit **5**

Reinforcement worksheet 2

1 If … we call it/them …

1 a bag is made of paper, a paper bag.

2 shoes are made of leather, leather shoes.

3 a toy is made of plastic, ________________.

4 keys are made of metal, ________________.

5 a ring is made of silver, ________________.

6 a box is made of cardboard, ________________.

7 bottles are made of glass, ________________.

8 a crown is made of gold, ________________.

9 sweaters are made of wool, ________________.

2 Number the pictures.

3 What is it? Read the description and use the code.

It is made of wood. It is in your classroom and in your house.
And you use it every day when you write and eat!

A	B	C	D	E	F	G	H	I	J	K	L	M	N	O	P	Q	R	S	T	U	V	W	X	Y	Z
1	2	3	4	5	6	7	8	9	10	11	12	13	14	15	16	17	18	19	20	21	22	23	24	25	26

_   _ _ _ _ _ _   _ _ _ _ _

1   23 15 15 4 5 14   20 1 2 12 5

Unit 5

Extension worksheet 1

1 Complete the sentences and cross out the materials on the wall.

1 Bottles are usually made of plastic or ___glass___ .

2 We get ____________ from sheep.

3 This worksheet is made of ____________ .

4 Paper and cardboard are made from ____________ !

5 The word ____________ comes from the names of two cities: New York and London.

6 Fur comes from animal ____________ .

7 Gold and silver are two types of ____________ .

8 Castles were often made of ____________ , wood, or brick.

9 Glass is made from a kind of ____________ .

10 Very warm clothes can be made of wool or ____________ .

11 Pens and rulers are usually made of ____________ .

~~glass~~	hair	stone	bone
sugar	oil	chocolate	fur
paper	wool	plastic	nylon
wood	metal	rubber	sand

2 Which four crossed out materials form a line? Write three things you can make with each of them.

1 ____________ : ____________ ____________ ____________

2 ____________ : ____________ ____________ ____________

3 ____________ : ____________ ____________ ____________

4 ____________ : ____________ ____________ ____________

Unit 5

Extension worksheet 2

10 Listen to Daisy. She's talking to her teacher. Color the things you hear in the picture and write.

Unit 5

Song worksheet

1 **11** **Listen and read. Write 8 of the things in verses 2, 3, and 4.**

1 a metal chair

2 ______

3 ______

4 ______

5 ______

6 ______

7 ______

8 ______

1 Everything's material,
Everything we see.
From rocks, plants, or animals,
Or from a factory.

2 This chair is made of metal,
That bowl is made of glass.
This table's made of wood,
And that skirt's made of grass.

3 This box is made of silver,
That watch is made of gold.
This scarf is made of wool,
And I wear it when it's cold.

4 Books are made of paper,
Their covers are made of cardboard.
Some things are made of plastic
That can be strong and hard.

2 **Draw three things from the song. Color and label them.**

______ ______ ______

Unit 5

Topic worksheet

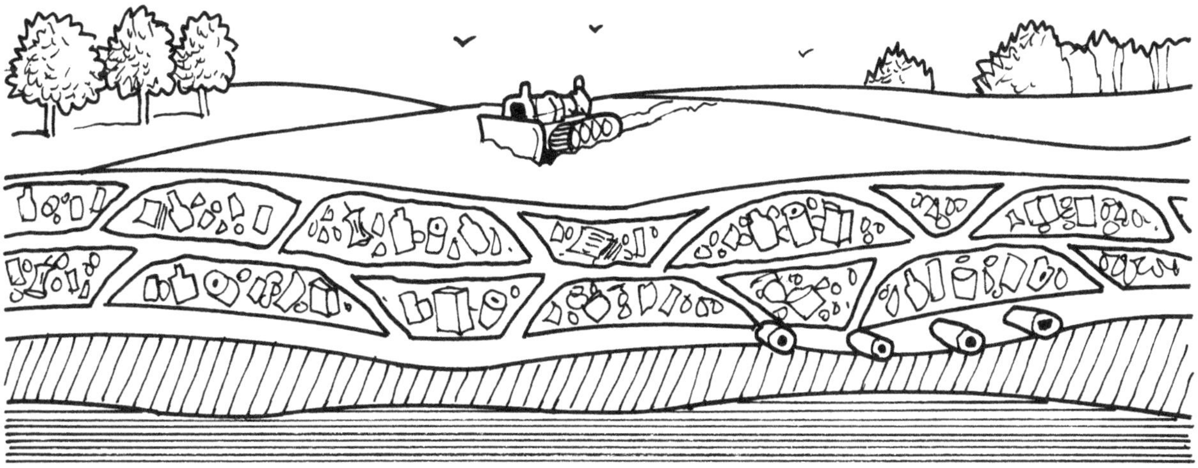

Landfill – a place where garbage is buried underground

1 Read about landfills. Underline 3 interesting facts.

Imagine you are an archeologist, but not one like Diggory Bones. He digs up bones and studies people from a long time ago. You study our garbage now! Every day we throw away a lot of things, like paper, metal, plastic, and grass. So you dig up the places where we put our garbage, *landfills*, to see what's inside!

Would you like to look at our garbage under the ground? It's very interesting. When one archeologist dug up landfills in the U.S.A., he found some old newspapers. He was surprised because they were 30 years old, but he could still read them! He also found five hot dogs. But he didn't eat them!

The archeologist found out that some things take much longer to decompose than he thought. He found grass, for example, that was not yellow. It was still green after many years.

This is a problem. There isn't very much more space underground for our garbage. We put a lot of paper in landfills. This is crazy, because it is easy to recycle. If we recycle paper, there's more space underground for things we can't recycle. So please don't throw paper away!

2 Make a list of ten things that you and your family threw away this week.

-- --

-- --

-- --

-- --

-- --

6 Teacher's notes

Reinforcement worksheet 1

- Tell students that it is Mary's birthday and her friends are playing a game. She is blindfolded and she has to guess what her presents are. Students read the three dialogs and complete the sentences, using the words in each cake.

Key: 1 sounds, What, bottle, 2 like, soft, feels, look, 3 Smell, smells, does, tastes.

- ***Optional follow-up activity:*** Students practice the dialogs in groups of four.

Reinforcement worksheet 2 F toward

- Students check the words that they see in the drawing. They then read the clues and write in the food words.

Key: 1) Words not checked should be: spoon, sausage, salt, onions. **2)** 2 salt, 3 spoon, 4 pepper, 5 knife, 6 fork, 7 olives, 8 meal.

- ***Optional follow-up activity:*** Students draw, color, and label their favorite meals. You could make a chart showing which meals are most/least popular in the class and stick their pictures around it. You may need to help them with some more food vocabulary.

Extension worksheet 1

- Students describe the clouds, using the expression *look(s) like*. Then students match the questions and answers. Point out: *feel like / smell like / taste like / sound like.*

Key: 1) (possible answers) 1 boat, 2 like a bottle, 3 This cloud looks like an elephant, 4 This cloud looks like a shoe. **2)** 2 What does it taste like? 3 What does it feel like? 4 What does it sound like? 5 What does it smell like? 6 What does it feel like?

- ***Optional follow-up activity:*** Students draw pictures of clouds and show them to their partner. What do they look like? Encourage students to use their imagination! If possible, bring in different smelling, tasting, and feeling objects. Put them in a bag or blindfold students if they are food, for them to describe what they smell, feel, taste, sound like, etc.

Extension worksheet 2

- Students read the steps for making a sandwich and put them in order. Then students write down six steps for making their favorite kind of sandwich. Ask them to cut along the dotted lines and give all of their sentences mixed up to their partner. The partner puts the steps in order.

Key: 4, 6, 2, 5, 3, 1, 7.

- ***Optional follow-up activity:*** Students put their sandwich recipes on the wall. They read each other's recipes and choose their favorite one. Suggest that for homework they make one of their friends' favorite sandwiches. What does it taste like?

Song worksheet

- Students match the words to the pictures and then write the words in the blanks. They listen to the song to check their answers.

Key: 1) Clockwise from example: a, f, d, n, c, i, k, g, h, m, b, l, e, j. **2)** See Student's Book, page 57.

- ***Optional follow-up activity:*** Students invent actions to go with the song and perform them while singing.

Topic worksheet

- Students read about animal senses and find three ways in which humans' senses are different. Students color the boxes containing things we eat and drink with red, food words green, drinks words blue, and the senses yellow. The picture will reveal a red flower on grass with a blue sky and a sun on the top right. Note: The picture is blurred or unclear because insects can't see shapes of objects as clearly as humans can.

Key: Human senses are different because we touch with our fingers, not our noses, we can't hear very high sounds, we can't smell danger like some animals, our eyes see differently.

Color code: green (food) – eggs, tomato, salt, cheese, salad, meat, bread; blue (drinks) – water, juice, milk, cola; red (things we eat and drink with) – knife, fork, spoon, bowl, plate, glass; yellow (senses) – touch, taste, hearing.

- ***Optional follow-up activity:*** Students discuss what is the most important sense for them and why.

Unit 6

Reinforcement worksheet 1

It's Mary's birthday. Her friends are playing a game. She has to guess what her presents are. Complete the sentences.

1

Sue: Mary! Listen to this! What does it ___sound___ like?

Mary: Mmmm. It ________ like water.

Sue: Now smell it! ________ does it smell like?

Mary: It smells like flowers! I think it's a ________ of perfume.

2

Peter: It's my turn. Touch this! What does it feel ________?

Mary: It feels like a ________ bowl.

Peter: But it's not a bowl! You put it on your head!

Mary: It ________ like a hat. Is it a hat?

Peter: Yes it is! And you're going to ________ like a movie star in it!

3

John: ________ this! What is it, Mary?

Mary: It ________ like chocolate.

John: Now taste it! What ________ it taste like?

Mary: It ________ creamy. It's a cake. I know, it's my birthday cake!

John: Yes, it is! And here's a fork and a plate, so you can eat it!

Unit 6

Reinforcement worksheet 2

1 Check (✓) the things that you can see in Amy's meal.

- fork ✓
- flour ☐
- spoon ☐
- sausage ☐
- cheese ☐
- pepper ☐
- salt ☐
- tomato ☐
- onions ☐
- pizza ☐
- plate ☐
- knife ☐
- olives ☐

2 Read the clues and write the words.

1 It's made of wheat. We use it to make bread and pizza. f l o u r

2 It's white and you use it to make your food taste good. _ _ _ _

3 It's something we use to eat soup and cereal. _ _ _ _ _

4 It's black and it tastes strong. _ _ _ _ _ _

5 It's made of metal. We use it to cut our food. _ _ _ _ _

6 They're small green or black fruits, and they taste strong. _ _ _ _

7 We put food on it when we eat. _ _ _ _ _

8 It's what we call breakfast, lunch, and dinner. _ _ _ _

Unit 6

Extension worksheet 1

1 Look at the clouds. They have interesting shapes. What do you think each one looks like?

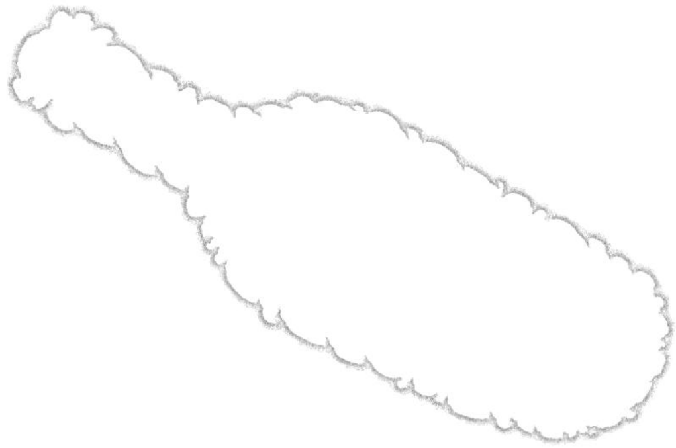

1 This cloud looks like a ....

....

2 This cloud looks ....

....

3 ....

....

4 ....

....

2 Complete the questions and the answers.

   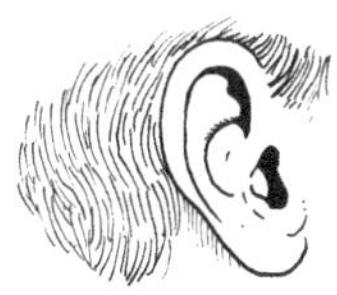

1 What ....does it smell.... like? It ....smells like a.... flower.

2 What .... like? It .... sugar.

3 What .... like? It .... fur.

4 What .... like? It .... French.

5 What .... like? It .... paint.

6 What .... like? It .... plastic.

Unit 6

Extension worksheet 2

1 This is how I make my favorite sandwich. Number the steps.

---------- Then I spread strawberry jelly, on top of the peanut butter.

---------- Then I cut them in half.

---------- First I take two pieces of bread.

---------- Then I put the two pieces of bread together.

---------- Next, I put peanut butter on both pieces of bread.

---------- Ingredients: two pieces of bread, strawberry jelly, and peanut butter.

---------- Finally, I eat my sandwich!

2 Write down six steps for making your favorite kind of sandwich. Then cut along the dotted lines and give all of your sentences to your partner. Ask your partner to put the steps in order.

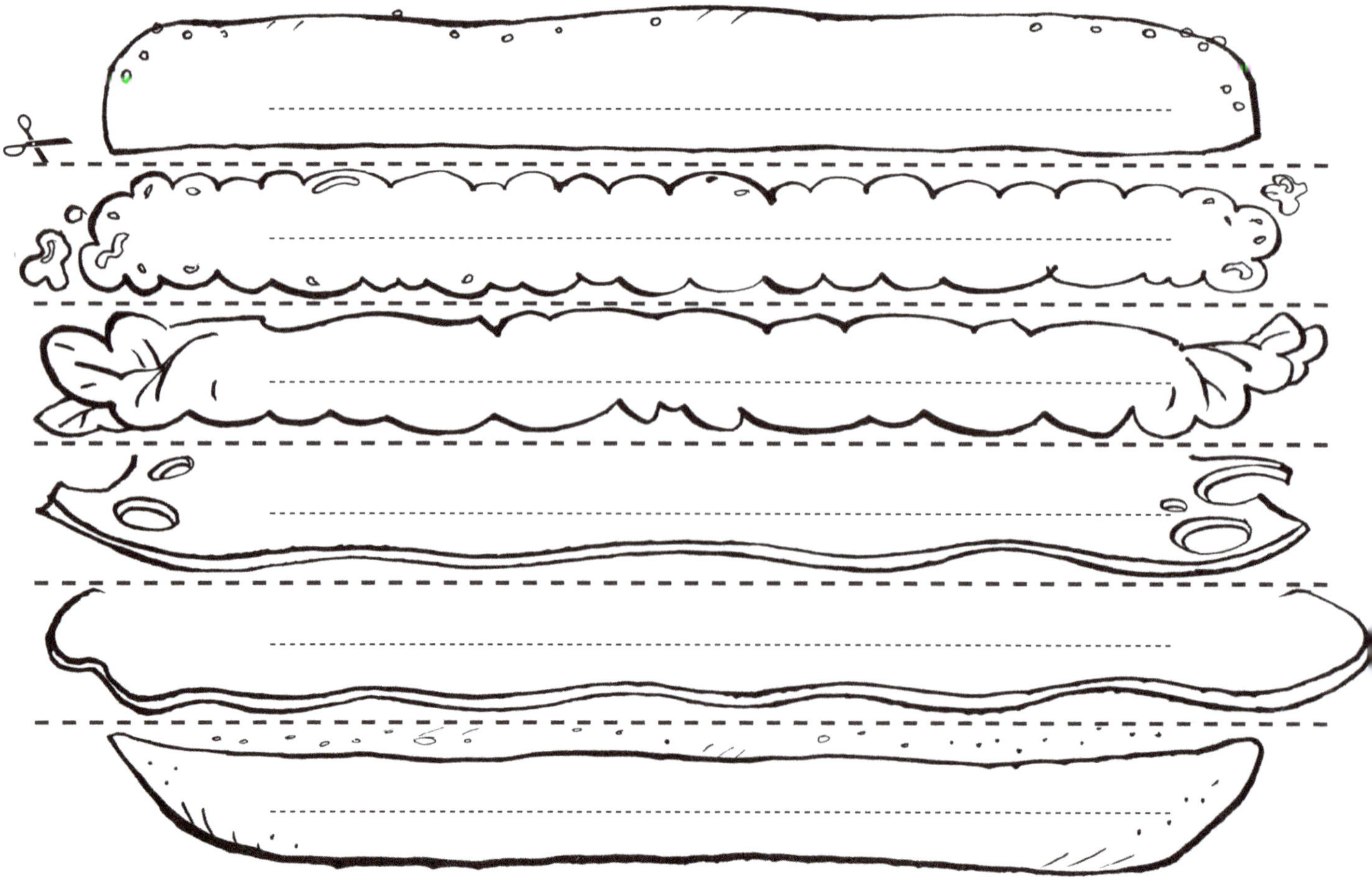

Unit 6

Song worksheet

1 Match the words with the pictures.

a ~~Mario~~	b wait	c cheese	d onion	e plate	f throw	g tastes
h hair	i knife	j hands	k bowl	l flour	m pizza	n listen

2 Complete the song with the words.

a

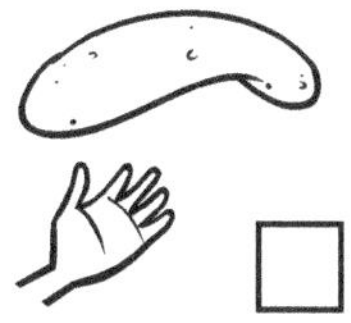

My name's Mario ,
I'm an Italian cook.
If you want to make a p.............. ,
Then l.............. to me and look.

Take salt, yeast, f.............. , and water,
Put them in a b.............. .
Mix them all together,
And w.............. for it to grow.

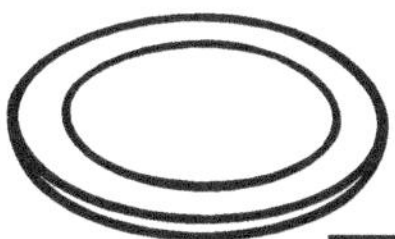

When the base is bigger,
Th.............. it in the air.
Use your h.............. to turn it,
Don't get it in your h.............. .

Now you choose your topping,
Tomato, pepper, and ch.............. .
You can choose anything,
Sausage, o.............. , and meat.

Cook for 15 minutes,
Then put it on a p.............. .
Cut it with a k.............. and fork,
Hmm. Now that .... great!

3 (12) Listen to the song and check your answers.

Unit 6

Topic worksheet

Read about the senses. Find three ways in which our senses are different from those of animals.

The Five Senses

The five senses are: touch, taste, hearing, smell, and sight. Humans usually have all five senses, but they are not the same as the senses of other animals. Think about touch. Humans touch things with their fingers, but small animals touch with their noses. What about taste? Snakes can taste food better than us! And hearing? Bats and dogs can hear very high sounds that humans can't hear. And humans can't smell danger like some animals. We can smell meat, but lions can smell it much better. They need to find and eat it!

Now think about sight. Humans see objects very differently from insects. Insects can't see objects very well. Their eyes are different from our eyes because they need to see movements and colors that we don't need. What does a red flower look like to you? To find out what a red flower looks like to an insect, color all the boxes with things we eat with and drink with in red in the picture. Now color the boxes with types of food in green. This is what green grass looks like to an insect.

Now color the drinks boxes in blue and the senses in yellow. These are what the sun and the sky look like to an insect.

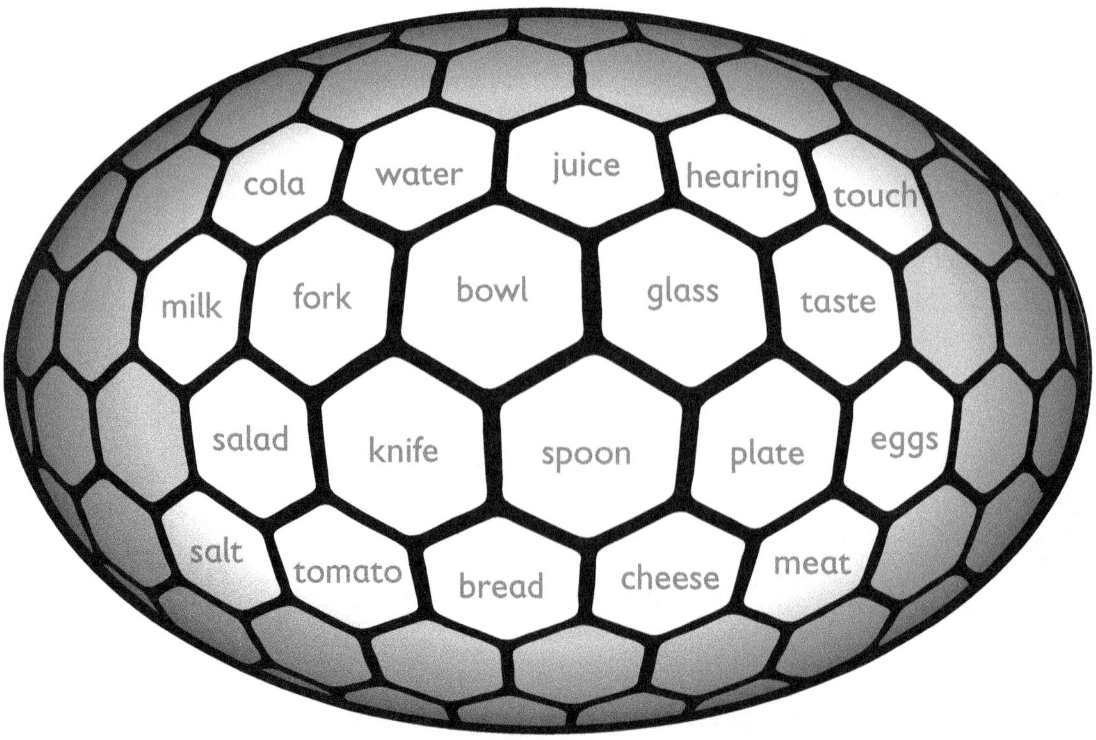

Reinforcement worksheet 1

- Students complete the statements and questions using *should(n't)* + the verb given in parentheses. Show students how to match the responses to these sentences by pointing out the example. They can then match the rest of the sentences on their own.

Key: 1) 2 should you do, 3 Should we run? 4 shouldn't walk, 5 shouldn't camp, 6 Should I tell, 7 should we put, 8 should we call? **2)** b 1, c 4, d 3, e 7, f 2, g 6, h 5.

- ***Optional follow-up activity:*** Students work in pairs and think about what they should do to keep themselves well and safe, for example, in the street or in the house. They make posters to put on the classroom wall for a *Keep Safe* campaign, using *should / shouldn't* sentences.

Reinforcement worksheet 2

- Students complete the sentences. They can refer back to the Student's Book, page 66 to help them. Then they copy the letters they have written in the boxes to find a ten-letter mystery word.

Key: 1) 2 Nature, 3 extinct, 4 wings, 5 Butterflies, 6 spots, 7 striped, 8 species, 9 insects, 10 collect. **2)** The mystery word is **rainforest**.

- ***Optional follow-up activity:*** Give a 10-minute time limit. In pairs or alone, students make as many words as they can out of *endangered species*. The words have to be a minimum of four letters long. They should not use plurals.

Extension worksheet 1

- Ask students if they know a nature park and introduce *The Bear Nature Park*. Elicit what students think you can do there. Explain that water fell on the instructions for visiting this park. Students read the instructions and fill in the missing words. Then they circle the eight words in the word search puzzle.

Key: 2 thirsty, 3 hat, 4 garbage, 5 shouldn't, 6 wings, 7 stripes, 8 your.

- ***Optional follow-up activity:*** Students write a set of instructions for a trip to the beach or the rainforest.

Extension worksheet 2 F toward

- Photocopy the worksheet and cut each worksheet in half. Introduce the two types of butterflies and tell students that they are going to tell their partner some information about them. Write the prompts from the worksheet on the board and elicit the full questions: *What color is your butterfly? How big are its wings? Where does it live? Can you tell me an interesting fact about your butterfly?* Ask students to sit in pairs, facing each other. Give one student in each pair the "Student A" sheet and the other one "Student B." As this is an information exchange activity, tell them they should not look at each other's sheets. Students focus on the Zebra Swallowtail first. Student As ask the questions and write down Student Bs' answers. Then students change roles. Students then color in the butterfly they have learned about using the information they've been given.
- ***Optional follow-up activity:*** Write useful words from the text without vowels on the board and ask students to come up and write the correct words e.g., *wng, spts, strps, bttrfly.* Students can then take turns writing up other words from the unit without vowels for the class to complete.

Song worksheet

- Students decide on actions to go with each line of the song. Get them to demonstrate some of their "moves" to the class. Play the song once and let them read the words and do the actions while they listen. Then play the song again. This time they have to listen only and do the appropriate actions, singing at the same time, if they can.
- ***Optional follow-up activity:*** Students work in pairs. They mime a line for another pair who have to guess the line from the song.

Topic worksheet

- Pre-teach: *camouflage, feathers, tail, pattern, poison, hide, polar bear, leaves, feel sick,* and *caterpillar.* Students read the article about camouflage. As they read, they choose a title for each paragraph. Then students look at the three pictures and talk or write about them. Help students by asking questions like: *What kind of animal is it? What color is it? Can you describe its pattern? How does it hide from its enemies? What does the enemy think it is? What kind of camouflage does it use? (Color, pattern, smell/poison, or all three?)*

Key: 1) 1 Color, 2 Pattern, 3 Smells and poison.
2) butterfly – pattern and color; caterpillar – pattern, color, smells; frog – pattern, color, possibly poison.

- ***Optional follow-up activity:*** Ask students to research *animal camouflage* on the Internet. They should bring information on camouflage they have found to the next lesson and tell their classmates about it, either by speaking or writing. You can refer them to: http://animals.howstuffworks.com/animal-facts/animal-camouflage-pictures.htm

Unit 7

Reinforcement worksheet 1

1 Complete the sentences with *should* / *shouldn't* and the words in parentheses.

1 People ...shouldn't throw... (not/throw) plastic bags in the lake.

2 What .... you .... (do) if you have a terrible toothache?

3 Oh, no! There's a cow in the field. Is it going to come after us? .... we .... (run)?

4 Daisy's face is very red. She .... (not/walk) in this hot sun.

5 What's that man doing? He .... (not/camp) there.

6 I don't understand this English homework. .... I .... (tell) my teacher?

7 Where .... we .... (put) our garbage?

8 Oh, no! There's a fire! Who .... we .... (call)?

2 Find the answers to questions 1–8.

a Call the firefighters. Quick! Here's my cell phone! ....8....

b That's right. It's dangerous for the ducks and fish. ....

c You're right. She should put some sunblock on. ....

d No, don't run! Just don't walk too close to it. ....

e In the garbage can, of course! ....

f You should go to the dentist. ....

g Of course you should. She can help you. ....

h Yes. It's not safe to put the tent there. ....

Unit 7

Reinforcement worksheet 2

1 Complete each sentence with a word about the natural world.

1 Zebras have black and white s t [r] i p e s.

2 N [ ] _ _ _ _ is in danger because of people's actions.

3 Creatures, like the dinosaur, that die out are e _ _ [ ] _ _ _.

4 Birds have w _ [ ] _ _. They need them to fly.

5 B _ _ _ _ _ _ [ ] _ _ _ _ are beautiful. They can fly.

6 Many fish have round s _ [ ] _ _ on their body.

7 The Siberian tiger has a long s _ [ ] _ _ _ _ tail.

8 There are a thousand endangered s _ [ ] _ _ _ _ in the world.

9 Flies and beetles are examples of flying i _ [ ] _ _ _ _.

10 People should not c _ _ _ _ _ [ ] fish to have in their homes.

2 Write the letters from the boxes in 1–10 to find a place where frogs live!

Unit 7

Extension worksheet 1

1 These are the instructions for having a good and safe time in The Bear Nature Park. But some rain fell on them. Complete the instructions.

Welcome to The Bear Nature Park!

Please follow these simple instructions:

1. You should pack a lot of bottles of ___water___ in your bag.
2. If you become ________, drink a lot of water.
3. Wear your ________ when the sun is hot.
4. After your picnic, put your ________ in the garbage can.
5. You ________ throw plastic bags in the lake.
6. There are many spotted butterflies in the park. Please don't touch them. You can break their ________.
7. Lehmann's frogs have red ________ and they are poisonous. Don't touch them.
8. You should always stay with ________ friends!

Enjoy your visit to The Bear Nature Park!

2 Find and circle the 8 missing words.

s	t	r	i	p	e	s	r
d	l	o	o	h	s	g	u
r	a	t	s	t	r	n	o
e	f	s	t	h	s	i	y
t	a	h	r	p	e	w	s
a	e	g	a	b	r	a	g
w	t	h	i	r	s	t	y
t	n	d	l	u	o	h	s

Unit 7

Extension worksheet 2

Student A – Ask your partner about the Zebra Swallowtail butterfly and write the answers. Then answer your partner's questions about the Red Admiral butterfly.

Zebra Swallowtail butterfly

What color?	
How big / wings?	
Where / live?	
Interesting fact?	

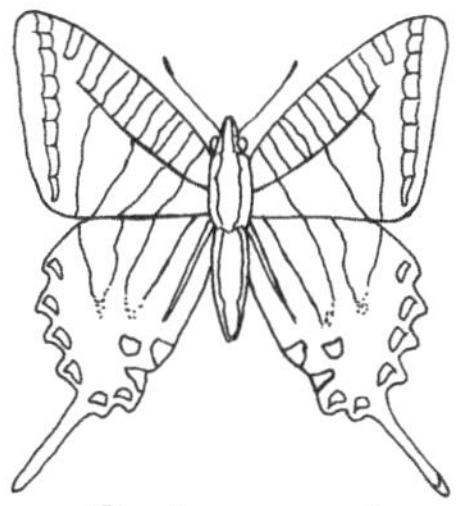

Color me!

Red Admiral butterfly

What color?	It's brown. It has white spots and red stripes.
How big / wings?	They're 6 cm long.
Where / live?	They live in yards and parks.
Interesting fact?	If they fly quickly in pairs, there is going to be a storm.

Student B – Answer your partner's questions about the Zebra Swallowtail butterfly. Then ask your partner about the Red Admiral butterfly and write the answers.

Zebra Swallowtail butterfly

What color?	It has black and white stripes. It has red and blue spots.
How big / wings?	They're 8 cm long.
Where / live?	They live close to rivers.
Interesting fact?	It has two long tails. Other animals think it's a bird.

Red Admiral butterfly

What color?	
How big / wings?	
Where / live?	
Interesting fact?	

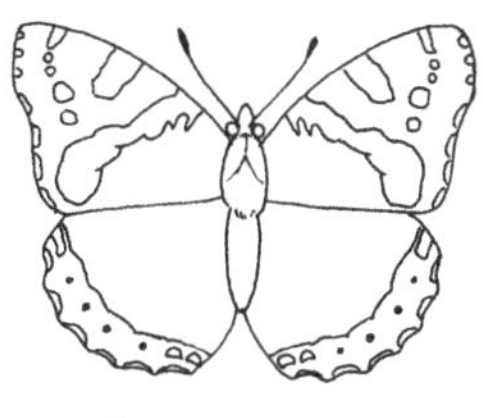

Color me!

Unit 7

Song worksheet

1 Listen and think of actions for each line of the song.

1 You shouldn't drop your garbage,
2 You should put it in a garbage can.
3 You shouldn't leave it on the ground,
4 You should clean up everything.
5 Here comes the bear, here comes the bear!
6 It's coming for your lunch!
7 Should I move or should I stop?
8 Should I climb that tree?
9 I should do something now.
10 That bear is after me.
11 You shouldn't go across the field,
12 You should walk around.
13 You shouldn't go too close to that cow,
14 It can push you to the ground.
15 You should run, you should run,
16 You should jump quickly.
17 Should I move or should I stop?
18 Should I climb that tree?
19 I should do something now.
20 That cow is after me!

2 Sing the song and do the actions.

Unit 7

Topic worksheet

1 Read about animal camouflage. Fill in the three titles.

Pattern **Smells and poison** **Color**

Imagine you are a small creature. You have a lot of enemies. People want to collect you. Animals want to eat or kill you. You cannot run quickly. So what should you do? Climb a tree? Run? No. You should hide – using camouflage. There are many types of camouflage:

1 ....

Many animals look like their natural home. Rabbits and other animals are brown, like the trees and the earth where they live. Many frogs are green, so they can hide in the green leaves. Polar bears have black skin but their white fur helps them hide in the snow or ice. Some animals can change the color of their fur or feathers in winter, fall, and summer.

2 ....

Different species have things on their fur, wings, tails, or feathers so that their enemies cannot see them very well or are afraid of them. For example, some butterflies have two big spots on their wings. The spots look like eyes. Enemies think that they are snakes and stay away. The Indian Leaf butterfly has wings that look like dead leaves. Enemies think the butterflies are plants and so they don't try to catch them.

3 ....

Birds and insects can catch caterpillars very easily because the caterpillars can't move quickly. So they have to make themselves taste or smell bad. Some caterpillars make a bad smell. The enemy doesn't like it and goes away. If enemies eat some kinds of frogs and butterflies, they feel sick or can die.

2 Look at the pictures. What camouflage do these animals use?

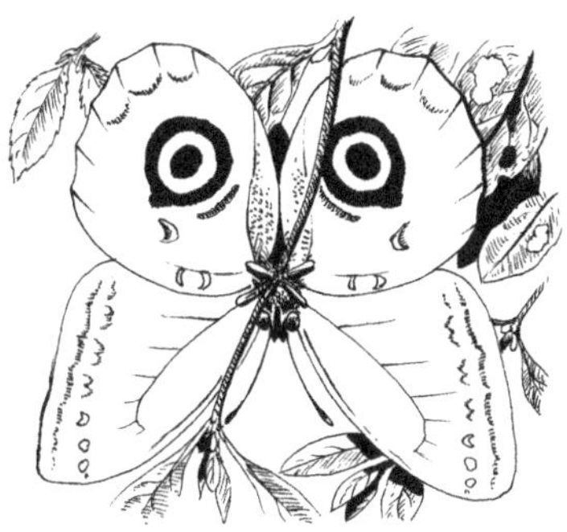

8 Teacher's notes

Reinforcement worksheet 1

- Students complete the questions with the correct past participle and then answer the questions to see what prize they've won.

Key: visited, won, stopped, not done, cooked, climbed, sailed, been, painted.

- ***Optional follow-up activity:*** Students work in pairs and design a similar game. They write ten new questions, using *Have you ever …* and add five new "prizes." Then they play the game!

Reinforcement worksheet 2

- Students use the code to find the first three letters of six sports and then write the full names of the sports. Then they fill in the blanks to complete which sport is done when.

Key: 1) 2 track and field, 3 sledding, 4 snowboarding, 5 skiing, 6 soccer. **2)** 2 soccer – fall and winter, 3 skiing – winter, 4 track and field – spring and summer, 5 snowboarding and sledding – winter.

- ***Optional follow-up activity:*** Students use the code to write the first three letters of other words from Unit 8 for their partners to figure out.

Extension worksheet 1

- Students complete the questions with *Have you ever … ?* and the verb. Then they read answers a–f and decide which question goes with each answer. Finally, students match the sports pictures to the questions/answers.

Key: 1) 2 Have you ever cycled in the Tour de France? 3 Have you ever run an important race in the winter? 4 Have you ever lost the ball? 5 Have you ever fallen through a hole in the ice? 6 Have you ever wanted to play a different sport? **2)** b 6, c 3, d 1, e 2, f 5. **3)** golf a4, cycling e2, ice skating f5, skiing d1, track and field c3, sledding b6.

- ***Optional follow-up activity:*** Write prompts on the board for several sports with appropriate collocating verbs such as: *go cycling, do track and field, go sledding, play field hockey.* Students copy them in the first column of a grid of five columns. At the top of the second column, they write *Me* and check or cross the sports they have and haven't done. Then they interview three students using *Have you ever … ?* questions and checking or crossing under their names in the three remaining columns.

Extension worksheet 2 F toward

- This activity mirrors the second part of the YLE Speaking Test. Students have to describe what's happening in the different pictures in a story. Ask questions to elicit useful vocabulary and pre-teach words like: *hole, ice, stuck, blade.* Students prepare their answers. In class, students work in pairs and talk about the pictures. Remind them that they should give as much detail as possible.
- ***Optional follow-up activity:*** Students imagine they were there when it happened. They write an email in the past tense to a friend, describing the event.

Song worksheet

- Students look at the pictures and fill in the missing words. Explain that sometimes *-ed* sounds like /t/ or /d/ (*walked, skied*) and sometimes *-ed* sounds like /ɪd/ (*snowboarded, needed*). Then students read the song and underline the verbs ending in *-ed*. Finally, they write the verbs in the correct pronunciation "goal net" and listen to the song to check their answers.

Key: 1) See Student's Book, page 75. **2)** /ɪd/: skated, /d/ /t/: played, skied, climbed, raced.

- ***Optional follow-up activity:*** Ask students to look back through the unit in the Student's Book and find past tense verbs ending in *-ed*. Write a list of them on the board. Students form small teams. Draw two *-ed* "goals" as on the worksheet. Say the words on the board one by one. Students write the word in the correct "goal" according to how the *-ed* ending is pronounced. Give students one point for each word in the correct net.

Topic worksheet

- Ask students how they feel when they haven't eaten for a while (tired, no energy). Explain that a *calorie* is a way to measure how much energy you get from food. Tell them that they are going to read about an *Olympic swimmer* named *Michael Phelps* who needs a lot of calories. Students read the text and underline the food words. They then check the pictures of foods that are in the text. Finally, students work in pairs to answer the questions.

Key: 1) Food words – egg sandwiches, cheese, tomato, onions, two cups of coffee, an omelet, potatoes, bread with sugar, chocolate pancakes, a plate of pasta, ham and cheese sandwiches, drinks, pizza. **2)** Food he doesn't eat is: chicken, apples, ice cream, sausages, carrots. **3)** 1 2,000, 2 12,000, 3 because they use a lot of energy when they play sports.

- ***Optional follow-up activity:*** Students imagine they are a famous sportsperson. They write a short description of their sport, what they do every day, and how much they eat. e.g., *My name's ____________. I'm a famous ____________. I've won ____________ gold medals and I've ____________. To play my sport, I need to be in very good shape. So every day I ____________. Also, I burn a lot of energy in my sport, so I need to eat a lot of calories. Every day I eat ____________ and I drink ____________.*

Unit 8 Reinforcement worksheet 1

Use the words in parentheses to complete the "*Have you ever…*" questions. Then play the game with a partner! Which prize does your partner win?

Unit 8

Reinforcement worksheet 2

1 Use the code to find the first three letters. Then write the names of the sports.

1 6 – 9 – 5 field hockey

2 20 – 18 – 1 ....

3 19 – 12 – 5 ....

4 19 – 14 – 15 ....

5 19 – 11 – 9 ....

6 19 – 15 – 3 ....

2 Label the pictures. When do people usually play each sport?

1 We usually play field hockey in the fall and winter.

2 We usually play .... in .... and ....

3 We go .... in ....

4 We usually do .... in .... and ....

 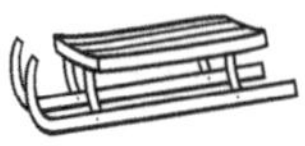 

5 We go .... and .... in ....

Unit 8

Extension worksheet 1

1 Complete these questions with *Have you ever* and the word in parentheses.

1 Have you ever had (have) an accident on a mountain?

2 ______ (cycle) in the Tour de France?

3 ______ (run) an important race in winter?

4 ______ (lose) the ball?

5 ______ (fall) through a hole in the ice?

6 ______ (want) to play a different sport?

2 Find the answers to questions 1–6.

a Yes. The balls I use are so small that they often get lost in trees or long grass. 4

b No, this sport is my favorite because you go very fast through the snow and it's safer than skiing. ______

c Yes, but in the winter we run inside so that it's not too cold. ______

d Yes, I hurt my leg last winter on Mont Blanc. ______

e No, but I want to ride my new racing bike in the next one. ______

f No, because I don't play my sport on frozen lakes. I play it on special ice rinks. ______

3 Decide which question and answer goes with each picture.

golf a4

cycling ☐

ice skating ☐

skiing ☐

track and field ☐

sledding ☐

Unit 8

Extension worksheet 2

Look at the pictures and think about the answers to the questions for each picture. Be ready to talk about the pictures.

1 What's the weather like? What are the children going to do? Where?

2 What are the children doing? What are they wearing? How do they feel?

3 What's happened to the little boy? Where is his foot?

4 What are the older children trying to do? What's happening to the ice?

5 Why has the girl taken her skate off? How is the little boy feeling?

6 How is the little boy getting out of the water? How is he feeling now?

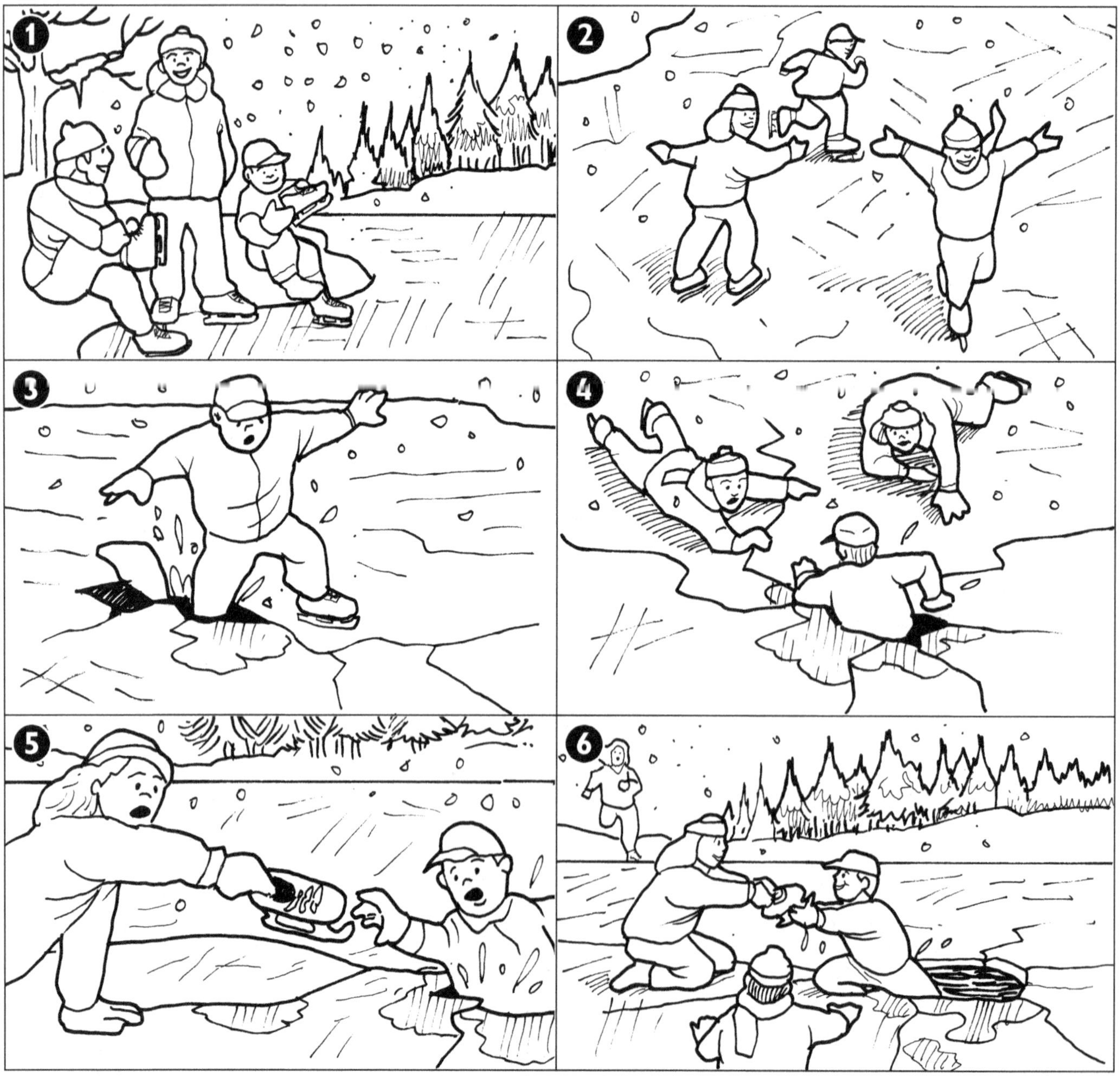

 Kid's Box AE Updated 2nd Ed. TRB 5

Song worksheet

1 Look at the pictures and complete the song.

We love sports, swimming, sailing, running,
We love sports,
We love to do it all.

We've skied down a ___mountain___ ,

We've __________ up a rock,

We've played __________ with Grandma,

We've raced against the __________ .

We've played __________ and tennis,

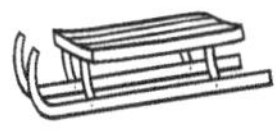

We've gone __________ in the snow,

We've skated in the __________ ,

We've made a __________ to throw.

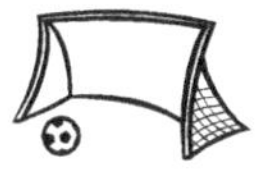

Some like playing ___soccer___ ,
Some like watching it.

It's good to move your __________ ,
DON'T JUST SIT!

2 Look at the example. Underline the other *-ed* words in the song and put them in the goals.

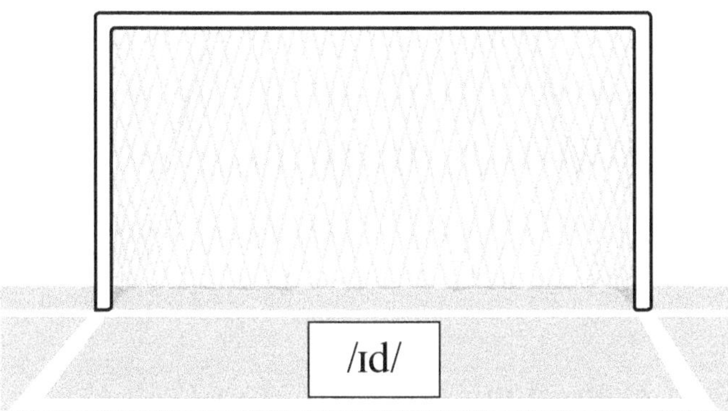

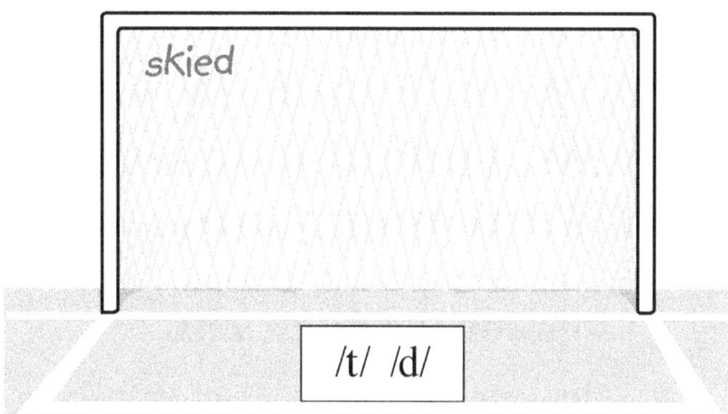

3 15 Listen and sing!

Unit 8

Topic worksheet

1 Michael Phelps is a famous Olympic swimmer. Underline all the foods he eats and drinks. Can you eat this much every day?

Most people only need about 2,000 calories every day, but Michael Phelps eats 12,000 calories a day. Every day!

Here is how Michael Phelps starts his day: three egg sandwiches topped with cheese, tomato, and onions. And that's before breakfast!

For breakfast, he has two cups of coffee, a five-egg omelet, a bowl of potatoes, three slices of bread with sugar on top, and three chocolate pancakes.

This famous swimmer's lunch is: a big plate of pasta and two large ham and cheese sandwiches on white bread. The best Olympic athlete in the history of the Olympic Games then completes his meal by drinking about 1,000 calories of drinks.

Dinner is two more plates of pasta and a whole pizza, that he eats with another 1,000 calories of drinks.

2 Check (✓) the pictures of foods that Michael Phelps eats. What *doesn't* he eat?

3 Answer the questions:

1 How many calories do most people need every day?

2 How many calories does Michael Phelps need every day?

3 Why do you think sports people need to eat so much?

Christmas worksheet 1

- To ensure that students understand the activity, read through the instructions together, and point out the first *job* word, *secretary*, that has been crossed out. Find one word in each of the other three categories. Students continue crossing out the words as instructed. Five words will be left (see key). To help students with this new vocabulary, they draw lines from the remaining five words to the pictures. Then students draw those five objects on the Christmas tree and color it.

Key: Job words – manager, actor, firefighter, teacher, dentist. Food words – cookies, olives, cake, pizza. Sound like *snow* – throw, go, know, so. Five words from left to right – stars, stocking, candles, fairy, presents.

- ***Optional follow-up activity:*** Students make a Christmas card using their picture of a tree. They stick their picture on the right-hand half of a piece of thin cardboard. They fold the left-hand half behind the picture and write a Christmas message inside. (For example: *I hope you have a wonderful Christmas* or *Merry Christmas!*)

Christmas worksheet 2

- Students read the jokes and talk about which ones they like best. Help them with useful vocabulary, such as: *reindeer, Santa Claus, paws, Dracula* (the blood-sucking vampire), *ice caps*. Use the illustrations to help with this. Then they cut each joke out, making sure to follow the dotted lines. They put the eight slips of paper in a pile, one on top of the other. (Note: the blank slip should be on the top of the pile.) They staple the left-hand side of the pile. Students then design the cover on the top slip of paper. They can label it *My Christmas Joke Book* and color it.
- ***Optional follow-up activity:*** Students make up some jokes of their own (or find more on the Internet). They can then write these jokes in their joke book (on the back of the existing jokes). If they write seven jokes, they could create a joke book that can be used in both directions – front to back, and back to front.

Easter worksheet 1

- Explain that, in many countries, it is traditional for children to *hunt* for real or chocolate eggs on Easter Day. The Easter Bunny *hides* the eggs. Ask students to look at the picture and spot the Easter eggs (there are three) and the Easter Bunny. Elicit vocabulary for things they can see in the picture, e.g., *bridge, river, path*. Students write instructions for the two children (who are in the left-hand corner), telling them how to find the Easter eggs. Finally students color the picture.

Key: 1) There are three Easter eggs. The Easter Bunny is behind the big tree. **2)** 1 Walk straight ahead. Turn left at the big tree. Walk down the river. There is a bridge on the left. Cross the bridge into the field of flowers. The egg is on the left, next to the bridge. 2 Walk straight ahead. Don't turn left or right when you see the big tree. Go straight ahead. There is a small house at the end of the path. The egg is under some trees on the right of the house. 3 Walk straight ahead. Turn right when you get to the big tree. Walk past the cave and go straight ahead. There is a small lake at the end of the path. The egg is across the lake. You can use the boat to get there!

- ***Optional follow-up activity:*** Students make an Easter card using their picture. They stick their picture on the right-hand half of a piece of thin cardboard. They fold the left-hand half behind the picture and write an Easter message inside (*Happy Easter!*)

Easter worksheet 2

- Students read the jokes. You will need to help them with the word plays, particularly for *hairbrush, hairspray, exercise, aerobics, hot cross buns* (a bread-based cake with a cross on top, eaten hot with butter at Easter.), e.g., pronunciation of *harebrush* sounds the same as *hairbrush*, *harerobics* sounds almost the same as *aerobics*. Students talk about which jokes they like best. Then they cut each joke out, making sure to follow the dotted lines. They put the eight slips of paper in a pile, one on top of the other. (Note: the blank slip should be on the top of the pile.) They staple the left-hand side of the pile. Students then design the cover on the top slip of paper. They can label it *My Easter Joke Book* and color it.
- ***Optional follow-up activity:*** Students write the question and answer for each joke on separate equally-sized pieces of card and play *Pelmanism* with them. Refer to the rules of *Pelmanism* in the Optional follow-up activity for Unit 1, Extension worksheet 1.

Christmas worksheet 1

1 Look at the lists of words and follow the instructions.

Cross out all the words that are jobs. The first one is done for you.
Cross out all the words that are kinds of food.
Cross out all the words that sound like *snow*.
Cross out the words *We wish you a Merry Christmas.*
What other five words about Christmas can you see?
Draw lines from the last five words to the pictures.

~~manager~~	go	candles	you
We	stocking	cake	a
stars	wish	know	presents
throw	firefighter	teacher	so
cookies	Merry	fairy	pizza
actor	olives	Christmas	dentist

2 Now decorate the Christmas tree with pictures of the five Christmas words.

Christmas worksheet 2

1 Read these Christmas jokes. Which ones do you like best?

What do snowmen wear on their heads?	*Ice caps!*
What did Dracula say at the Christmas party?	*Would you like a bite?*
What do snowmen eat for lunch?	*Icebergers!*
Who takes presents to cats at Christmas?	*Santa Paws!*
What's the best thing to put in a Christmas cake?	*Your teeth!*
What's the best thing to give your friends for Christmas?	*A list of everything you want!*
What do you call a reindeer with a fur hat?	*Anything you want – he can't hear you!*

2 Make your own joke book! First, cut around the edge of each joke. Next put the jokes in a pile. Then staple them together on the left and design the cover.

Easter worksheet 1

1 **John and his sister Sue are looking for Easter eggs. How many Easter eggs can you see? Where is the Easter Bunny?**

2 **Help John and Sue to find the Easter eggs. Complete the directions.**

1 Walk straight ahead. Turn left at the big tree. Walk down the river. There is a bridge on the left. Cross

2

3

3 **Now color the picture.**

Easter worksheet 2

1 Read these Easter jokes. Which ones do you like best?

Why isn't the Easter Bunny fat?	*Because he does a lot of eggsercise!*
How does Easter end?	*With the letter R!*
What happens if you pour hot water on bunnies?	*You get hot cross bunnies!*
How does the Easter Bunny stay in good shape?	*He does a lot of harerobics!*
How does the Easter Bunny keep his hair nice?	*With a harebrush!*
What do you call a rabbit that tells good jokes?	*A funny bunny!*
How does a rabbit keep his fur looking good?	*With harespray!*

2 Make your own joke book! First, cut around the edge of each joke. Next put the jokes in a pile. Then staple them together on the left and design the cover.

Name: ....

Grade: ....

1 16 **Listen and draw lines. There is one example.**

2 **17** **Listen and write. There is one example.**

CHANNEL 3
needs TEENAGE ACTORS
for a new TV series!

	Full name:	Peter ......Clark......
1	**Age:**	....
2	**Favorite TV series:**	.... is Cool
3	**Favorite actor:**	Will ....
4	**Day to visit Channel 3:**	....
5	**Time:**	....

3 **18** **What is each student's favorite school subject? Listen and write a letter in each box. There is one example.**

Katy ☐

Ben E

Mary ☐

Bill ☐

Emma ☐

Tom ☐

A

B

C

D

E

F

G

H

4 19 Listen and check (✓) the box. There is one example.

Where's Ben's mom going to work?

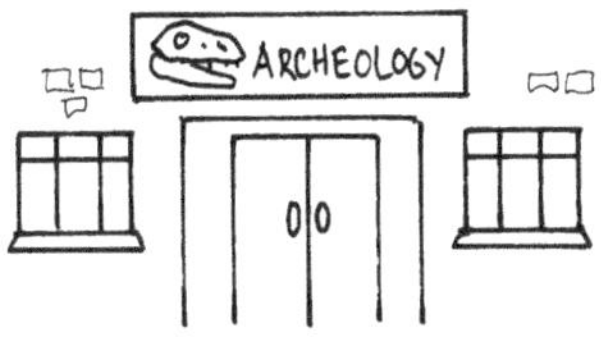

A ✓

B

C

1 What job is Ben's mom going to do?

A

B

C

2 Who's Ben's mom going to work for?

A

B

C

3 When's Ben's mom going to start her new job?

A

B

C

4 What kind of TV show is the School of Archeology going to be on?

A

B

C

5 What's Ben's mom's job now?

A

B

C

5 20 Listen and color and write. There is one example.

Test Units Welcome–2

Reading and Writing

Name: ....

Grade: ....

1 Look and read. Choose the correct words and write them on the lines. There is one example.

history		a reporter
the news		pilots
~~the weather~~		geography
a firefighter		cartoons
doctors		dentists
an ezine		science
a dictionary		a notebook

On this show, they tell you if it's going to be sunny, windy, or rainy. *the weather*

1 It's a kind of book. When we don't understand a word, we can use this. ....

2 These are TV shows for children. They're "moving pictures" and they're very funny. ....

3 This is a kind of job. When there is a fire, this person puts it out. ....

4 It's a school subject. In this class, we learn about plants and the human body. ....

5 These people wear a uniform. They fly airplanes. ....

6 If you like learning about the past, you should study this subject. ....

7 In this school subject, you can learn about different countries and people. ....

8 These people help you when you have a toothache. They clean your teeth, too. ....

9 This is a kind of TV show. You watch it when you want to know what is happening in the world. ....

10 This is something you read. It's a kind of internet magazine. Students write about interesting things in it. ....

2 Alex is talking to his teacher, Mrs. Hill. What does Mrs. Hill say? Read the conversation and choose the best answer. Write a letter (A–H) for each answer. You do not need to use all the letters.

Example

Alex: Excuse me, Mrs. Hill. Can I ask you some questions? It's for my ezine project.

Mrs. Hill: ...C...

Questions

1

Alex: You're an artist. Did you like art when you were in school?

Mrs. Hill: ....

2

Alex: Where do you usually paint?

Mrs. Hill: ....

3

Alex: Do you like painting animals?

Mrs. Hill: ....

4

Alex: What are you going to paint next?

Mrs. Hill: ....

5

Alex: Great. That's all. Thank you for your time, Mrs. Hill.

Mrs. Hill: ....

A A picture for my husband's birthday.

B At home. I have a special room there.

C Of course. What would you like to know? (***Example***)

D You're welcome, Alex. Good luck!

E At seven o'clock in the morning.

F Yes, I do. But I think people are more interesting.

G Yes, I did. It was my favorite subject.

H My husband's an artist, too!

3 **Read the story. Choose a word from the box. Write the correct word next to numbers 1–5. There is one example.**

example
~~School~~ quickly important happy library forty
run talk newspaper call

Yesterday Alex and Maria were at Park Road ...School........ .

They wanted to watch TV, so they looked at a (**1**) ....

A sports quiz was on TV at four o'clock. Alex and Maria love quizzes, but it was already three (**2**) .... !

So they started to run home (**3**) .... But when they ran through the park, they saw a fire.

Maria stopped running. "Come on!" Alex said. "We're late."

He was angry because he didn't want to miss the quiz. But Maria knew that it was dangerous to leave the fire.

"No, Alex. I'm going to (**4**) .... the firefighters," she said. Five minutes later the firefighters arrived. "Good job!" a firefighter told them. "You did the right thing." Alex felt good. He thought Maria was right. Putting out a fire was more (**5**) .... than a TV sports quiz.

(6) **Now choose the best name for the story. Check (✓) one box.**

The sports quiz ☐ A fire at the park ☐ Always leave a fire ☐

4 Read the text. Choose the right words and write them on the lines.

Learn to spell well

Example Are you good at learning to ...write... new words in your first language
1 or a second language? .... you know if *science* or *sceince* is the correct spelling in English? (It's *science*, of course.)

2 .... you are learning a second language, it is sometimes difficult to learn to spell new words and to remember the correct spelling. But
3 ....are a lot of things you can do to make this easier.

One very important thing is to buy a good dictionary or find an online
4 dictionary that you like .... You can also have a notebook where
5 you write down .... new word you learn. Another good idea is
6 to stick new words .... a wall in your house so you see the words
7 each day. You .... also read a lot of the books you enjoy, so you see a lot of different words without having to work very hard.

8 Some schools have spelling competitions. They are .... "Spelling Bees." The student who can spell the most words without any mistakes
9 .... a prize. These competitions help children learn a lot of new
10 words. ....don't you have one in your English class?

Example	writing	write	writes
1	Are	Do	Canl
2	So	But	When
3	they	there	those
4	using	use	used
5	all	many	every
6	on	in	at
7	have	will	should
8	call	calling	called
9	win	winning	wins
10	How	Why	Where

5 Look at the picture and read the story. Write some words to complete the sentences about the story. You can use 1, 2, 3, or 4 words.

The music competition

Harry's favorite subject in school is music. He has music classes on Monday and Friday. He loves them. At home, he likes playing the guitar and singing, too. "You're going to be a great singer one day," his music teacher often tells him.

One day Harry's music teacher told him about a music competition. "In September there's going to be a very important competition with a big prize," she said. Harry was really interested. "I think you should sing in the competition," she told him. "But first you are going to need a lot of practice," she said. "Come to school early every morning and we can practice your songs before the other students arrive."

The next week Harry had to wake up at 6:00 every morning and leave the house at 6:30 to walk to school. He practiced singing with his music teacher, but he was really tired. Harry didn't like getting up early! And it was a lot of work. "Can you repeat that song, Harry?" she asked again and again.

At the competition he sang very well. But when he won the second prize, he was sad. "You said I'm going to be a great singer, but I didn't win," he told his teacher. "Harry, you did very well, but if you want to be a great singer, you have to work harder than all the other singers in the world," she said.

Examples

Music is Harry's ......favorite subject...... at school.

He enjoys singing and playing ......the guitar...... .

Questions

1 Harry's music classes are .... each week.

2 Harry's teacher thinks that one day Harry can be a ....

3 The competition was in the month of ....

4 Every morning of the next week Harry woke up at .... o'clock.

5 Harry walked to .... to practice with his music teacher.

6 He sang very .... at the competition.

7 At the competition he won the ....

6 Read the diary and write the missing words. Write one word on each line.

	Sunday
Example	This afternoon, I ...went... to John's house with Jen. We arrived at
1	quarter to four because we wanted to .... the cartoons on TV at four o'clock. But when we turned on the television, a sports program was on. "Oh, no! I hate golf!" said Jen. We tried the other channels, but there
2	were no cartoons on any of them. "What can we do now?" I .... John and Jen. Before they could answer, John's mom came into the room.
3	She .... a great idea. "Why don't you *make* a cartoon?" she said.
4	She is .... artist, and she showed us how to do it.
5	So we all made a cartoon. We drew a lot .... pictures. It was a really amazing afternoon!

7 Look at the three pictures. Write about this story. Write 20 or more words.

1

Teacher's card

Find the Differences

Student's card

Find the Differences

2

Teacher's card

Nick

How / old / Nick	?
Documentaries interesting / boring	?
Hobbies	?
How many brothers and sisters	?
Going to be	?

Jenny

How / old / Jenny	12
Documentaries interesting / boring	interesting
Hobbies	playing soccer, swimming
How many brothers and sisters	three
Going to be	a scientist

Find Information. Ask and answer.

Student's card

Nick

How / old / Nick	13
Documentaries interesting / boring	boring
Hobbies	playing the guitar, singing
How many brothers and sisters	two
Going to be	a computer science teacher

Jenny

How / old / Jenny	?
Documentaries interesting / boring	?
Hobbies	?
How many brothers and sisters	?
Going to be	?

Find Information. Ask and answer.

3 The science test

Tuesday

Michael

Tuesday

Wednesday

Thursday

Friday

Tell the Story

Test Units 3–4

Listening

Name: ....

Grade: ....

1 21 **Listen and draw lines. There is one example.**

Anna Kim Helen Robert

Bill Michael Jack

2 Listen and write. There is one example.

Welcome to London!

	Name:	Sarah Perez
1	**Age:**	....
2	**Staying at:**	The .... Hotel
3	**In London with:**	....
4	**Days in London:**	Monday through ....
5	**Name of toy store:**	....

3 **23** **What happened to the students in Robert's class? Listen and write a letter in each box. There is one example.**

Mary ☐

Vicky [F]

Alex ☐

Jane ☐

William ☐

David ☐

A

B

C

D

E

F

G

H

4 24 Listen and check (✓) the box. There is one example.

Where in town was the fire?

A ✓

B ☐

C ☐

1 Where was the café?

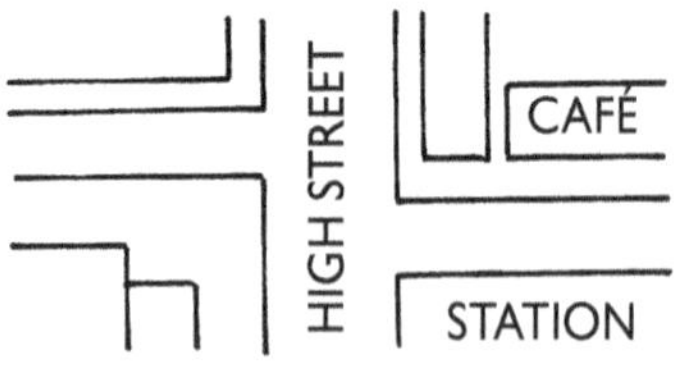

A ☐

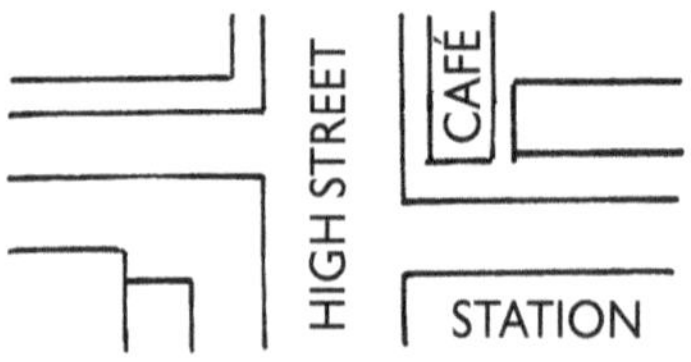

B ☐

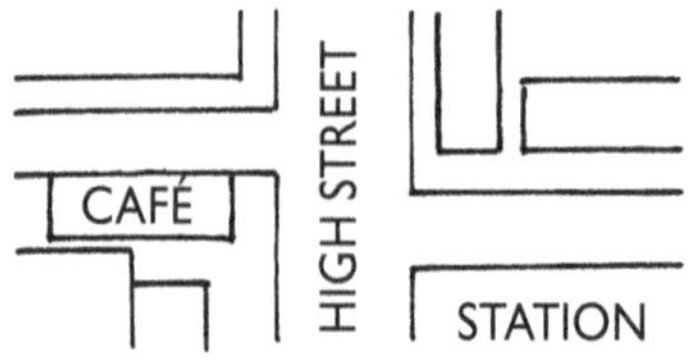

C ☐

2 Where did the fire start?

A ☐

B ☐

C ☐

3 What was Mr. Green doing when the fire started?

A ☐

B ☐

C ☐

4 What did the customers do when the fire started?

A ☐

B ☐

C ☐

5 Where did the man hear about the fire?

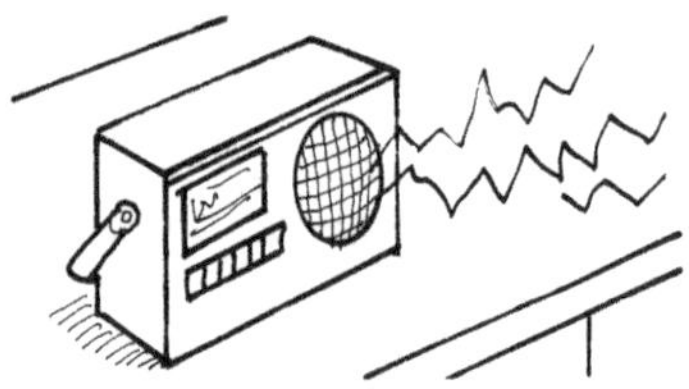

A ☐

B ☐

C ☐

5 25 **Listen and color and write. There is one example.**

Test Units 3–4

Reading and Writing

Name: ....

Grade: ....

1 Look and read. Choose the correct words and write them on the lines. There is one example.

fire stations December July

a castle October

an airport a factory

February a bridge

museums a bank

hotels a stadium

~~a skyscraper~~ January

This is a very tall building with a lot of floors. ......a skyscraper......

1 If you want to cross a river, you walk over this. ....

2 It's a really strong building. The Queen lives in one. ....

3 This is a month. It's the one after September. ....

4 People don't live in these buildings. Firefighters work in them. ....

5 Christmas is in this month. It's the last month of the year. ....

6 These buildings have a lot of interesting things to see. The "Rosetta Stone" is in one. ....

7 This month is between June and August. ....

8 This is a place where you can catch a plane. ....

9 In this place in town you can get money. ....

10 This is the shortest month in the year. In most years it only has 28 days. ....

2 **Luke is at the zoo, but he can't find the penguins. He asks a zoo keeper, Rachel, for help. What does Rachel say?**
Read the conversation and choose the best answer.
Write a letter (A–H) for each answer.
You do not need to use all the letters.

Example

Luke: Excuse me. Can you help me?

Rachel: ....C....

Questions

1

Luke: Are there any penguins here, please?

Rachel: ....

2

Luke: Can you tell me where the penguins are?

Rachel: ....

3

Luke: What do penguins like to eat?

Rachel: ....

4

Luke: Where can I buy some?

Rachel: ....

5

Luke: I'm going to get some for the penguins' dinner.

Rachel: ....

A Fish. They swim really fast and catch them in the water.

B I love them, too.

C Yes, of course. (***Example***)

D I'll show you on the map – go down this path and turn left at the big tree.

E The produce market? Take the third street on the right.

F Not here at the zoo. Maybe from the market.

G But you can't feed the animals in the zoo!

H Yes, the zoo has a great penguin area with a large pool.

3 **Read the story. Choose a word from the box. Write the correct word next to numbers 1–5. There is one example.**

example
~~dad~~ minutes fall most paintings across more corner feel bridge

Last July, Sarah went on vacation with her mom and *dad*. On the first morning, they went to an art museum to look at some (**1**) .... They walked for hours. At one o'clock, they were tired and hungry. So they decided to go and eat something.

There was a restaurant (**2**) .... the street, where Sarah ate a big pizza and drank some cola.

After lunch, they visited an old castle. It was one of the (**3**) .... beautiful castles in the country, on a hill above the river. Sarah and her parents loved it.

But when they were leaving, the ground suddenly started to move. It moved for about two (**4**) .... and then it stopped. "What was that?" Dad asked. "I think it was an earthquake!" said Mom. "Don't worry," said Dad. "The buildings aren't going to (**5**) .... down." He was right. It was only a very small earthquake, but Sarah had some exciting news to tell her friends when she got home.

(6) **Now choose the best name for the story. Check (✓) one box.**

An exciting story ☐ Sarah's mom ☐ The castle on the hill ☐

4 **Read the text. Choose the right words and write them on the lines.**

The Titanic

Example The Titanic ___was___ the name of a very big ship.

1 In 1912 ________ famous ship had a terrible disaster. It was
2 ________ across the Atlantic Ocean from England to the U.S.A.
3 ________ April 14th when it hit an iceberg. No one saw the
4 iceberg because ________ was a lot of fog. Many people were
5 having dinner in the restaurant ________ sleeping when the water
6 ________ into the ship. Emily Haisman was only 15 years old.
7 She was safe. With many women and children she climbed ________
8 small boats and ________ in the ocean for help.
9 But ________ father and hundreds of other people died when
10 the ship sank. It was the ________ ship disaster in history.

Example	were	was	had
1	these	this	those
2	sailed	sail	sailing
3	on	by	at
4	it	there	they
5	or	when	but
6	coming	came	comes
7	under	into	through
8	waits	wait	waited
9	his	her	hers
10	worst	worse	bad

5 **Look at the picture and read the story. Write some words to complete the sentences about the story. You can use 1, 2, 3, or 4 words.**

The school visit

On Tuesday, May 4th the science teacher, Mrs. Wood, took the class to visit a science museum. It was an interesting museum, but Martin and his friends didn't like it. "This is boring," said Martin. When the science teacher wasn't looking, Martin and three friends ran to the park.

They played at the park for half an hour, but then they were bored again. It was only 11 o'clock. So they went to the river. "This is fun!" said Martin. But when he was playing by the water, he fell in. The river was moving very quickly, and he couldn't swim very well.

"Let's go and get the teacher," said Martin's friends. So they ran to the museum and found her. "Mrs. Wood! Please come quickly! Martin is in the river!"

The teacher ran to the river. She could swim very well, so she jumped in and helped Martin.

Martin was feeling terrible when he climbed out of the river. He was wet, cold, and sad. He said, "I'm sorry, Mrs. Wood. I was very naughty."

In June the class went to the city to visit the castle. This time Martin was good. He stayed next to the history teacher all the time.

Examples

...Tuesday May 4th... was the date that the class went to the science museum with Mrs. Wood.

Martin thought that the science museum was ...boring... , and he didn't like it.

Questions

1 Martin went with .... to the park.

2 At the park, they were bored after they played for ....

3 They left the park at .... in the morning.

4 Martin .... the river when he was playing near it.

5 It was difficult for Martin to .... because the river was moving quickly.

6 Martin felt .... when he came out of the water.

7 Martin's class went to a castle in the month of ....

6 Read the letter and write the missing words. Write one word on each line.

Dear Kate,

Example How are you? I hope you ....are.... well. I'm fine. We are

1 .... vacation! I'm visiting interesting places in the city. It's

2 really fun. But yesterday I .... a terrible day! I was trying to get to the museum and I got lost. The first person told me it was

3 two streets past the park. The .... person told me it was on the corner of 6th Street and 24th Street. The third person told

4 me it was next .... the fire station. Finally, I got so tired that I went back to the hotel!

5 Can you .... me where the museum is?

Love,

Jane

7 Look at the three pictures. Write about this story. Write 20 or more words.

1

Teacher's card

Find the Differences

Student's card

Find the Differences

2

Teacher's card

Mary

Where / go / this morning	?
Who / see	?
What / Queen / say	?
What time / Mary / leave	?
What / do / this afternoon	?

Richard

Where / go / this morning	fire station
Who / see	his uncle
What / uncle / say	"I'm going to show you my work."
What time / Richard / leave	1:55
What / do / this afternoon	play soccer at park

Find Information. Ask and answer.

Student's card

Mary

Where / go / this morning	castle
Who / see	Queen
What / Queen / say	"Would you like some tea?"
What time / Mary / leave	11:50
What / do / this afternoon	go to museum

Richard

Where / go / this morning	?
Who / see	?
What / uncle / say	?
What time / Richard / leave	?
What / do / this afternoon	?

Find Information. Ask and answer.

3 Fred loses his dog

Tell the Story

Test Units 5–6

Listening

Name: ....

Grade: ....

1 26 **Listen and draw lines. There is one example.**

Mary Sarah Harry Fred

Lucy Jim Alex

2 27 Listen and write. There is one example.

Katy's Party

	Name:	Katy Barker
1	**Having a party at:**	....
2	**Giving money to:**	"Help the ....”
3	**Katy's food:**	chocolate ....
4	**Number of people:**	....
5	**Telephone number:**	....

3 28 **What did the children in the class make? Listen and write a letter in each box. There is one example.**

Anna [D]

David [ ]

John [ ]

Sally [ ]

Katy [ ]

Richard [ ]

A

B

C

D

E

F

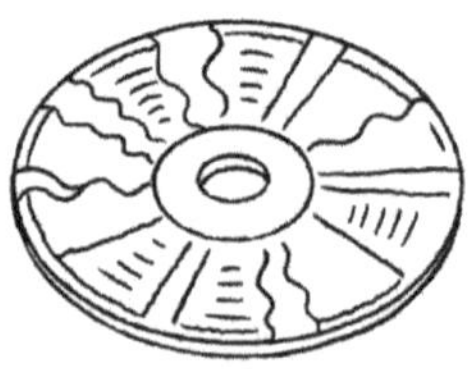
G

H

4 29 Listen and check (✓) the box. There is one example.

Where was Jason's birthday party?

A ☐

B ✓

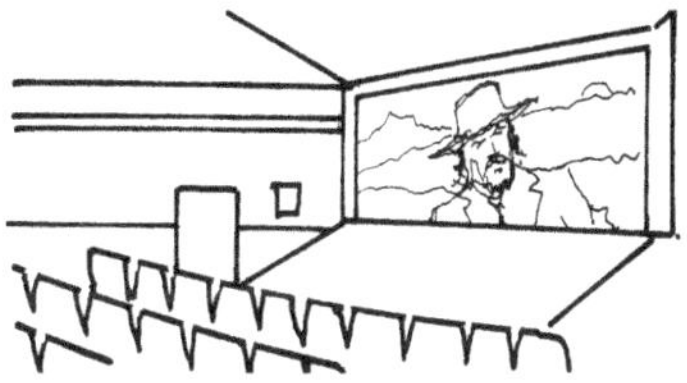
C ☐

1 Why didn't Grandma go to the birthday party?

A ☐

B ☐

C ☐

2 What did Jason eat?

A ☐

B ☐

C ☐

3 What did the birthday cake look like?

A ☐

B ☐

C ☐

4 What was Jason's favorite present?

A ☐

B ☐

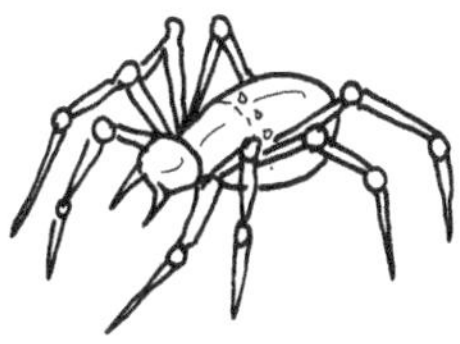
C ☐

5 When is Jason going to visit his grandparents?

A ☐

B ☐

C ☐

5 30 **Listen and color and write. There is one example.**

Test Units 5–6

Reading and Writing

Name: ....

Grade: ....

1 Look and read. Choose the correct words and write them on the lines. There is one example.

paper | a costume | meals | a bowl | a scarf | salt | spoons | a knife | ~~plastic~~ | pepper | wood | fur | glass | plates | gold

This material is made using oil. Cameras, bags, and computers are often made of it. ......plastic......

1. They're round. You put pizza and other food on them. ....
2. We eat three of these every day. The first one is breakfast. The last one is dinner. ....
3. This is a kind of material. It's very warm and it comes from animals. Hats are often made of it. ....
4. This material is made from trees. We write on it. There is a lot of it in your notebook. ....
5. This material can break easily. Bottles are usually made of it. ....
6. This makes food taste good. When you are cooking pasta, you put it into the water. ....
7. This is a kind of metal. It's expensive. Watches are sometimes made of it. ....
8. It's made of metal. You use it to cut bread and fruit. ....
9. It's made of wool and you wear it when it's cold. You put it around your neck. ....
10. These are often made of metal. You use them to eat soup and ice cream. ....

2 **Anne is bringing some materials to Mr. Green to be recycled. What does Anne say?**
Read the conversation and choose the best answer.
Write a letter (A–H) for each answer.
You do not need to use all the letters.

Example

Mr. Green: Can I help you, Anne?

Anne: C

Questions

1

Mr. Green: What do you want to recycle?

Anne: ....

2

Mr. Green: Put the plastic bottles in the blue bin.

Anne: ....

3

Mr. Green: The bin on the left is full.

Anne: ....

4

Mr. Green: Do you have any clothes to recycle?

Anne: ....

5

Mr. Green: It's really good that you recycle things, Anne. Good job.

Anne: ....

A What about the wood?

B Oh yes, I'll have to use the one on the right.

C Yes, please. I want to recycle some things. (***Example***)

D No, I don't. That's everything for today, Mr. Green.

E Some plastic bottles and some old newspapers.

F They're made of wool.

G OK. And I know the newspapers go in the red bins.

H Thank you. I think it's important.

3 **Read the story. Choose a word from the box. Write the correct word next to numbers 1–5. There is one example.**

example

~~mom~~ taste hungry soft sound feel look
terrible cold old

Beth was staying with her grandparents when her ....mom.......... called her. "I have a surprise for you. Guess what it is!" her mom said.

Beth and her mom often played this game. They asked questions about the five senses of smell, hearing, sight, touch, and **(1)** ....

Beth said, "OK. First question: "What does it **(2)** .... like? Is it pretty?" Mom said, "Yes. It's small and beautiful." Beth asked, "Is it a toy?" Mom said, "No. But you *can* play with it."

"OK. What does it feel like?" Beth asked. Mom said, "It feels **(3)** .... and warm."

Beth asked, "What does it taste like? Is it a cake?" Mom said, "You can't *eat* it!" Then Beth said, "I know! It's a cat!" Her mom said, "No, but it is a kind of animal."

Then Beth asked, "What does it **(4)** .... like?" Mom said, "Well, sometimes it's quiet and sometimes it's very noisy." "Is it a dog?" Beth asked but she was wrong again.

"OK. Fifth sense, Mom," said Beth "What does it smell like?"

Mom said, "Well, sometimes it smells nice and sometimes it smells **(5)** ....!"

"I know," said Beth. "It's a new baby!"

Mom said, "Yes, it's your new baby sister! And she's two days old!"

(6) **Now choose the best name for the story. Check (✓) one box.**

A new person in the family ☐ Beth's new cat ☐ Something good to eat ☐

4 Read the text. Choose the right words and write them on the lines.

Banana bread recipe

Example Many people all over the world like to ......eat...... bread.

1 Bread is a very healthy food .... it gives people energy

2 .... work, play, or study.

3 It's easy to .... delicious banana bread.

4 First, ... mix the butter and sugar in a big bowl. Then

5 you add .... egg and some mashed bananas. Next,

6 .... another bowl, mix flour, baking soda, and salt.

7 After that, mix the dry ingredients .... the wet ones.

8 Put the banana bread in the oven and bake it for .... hour.

9 Finally, ... the banana bread out of the oven and cut it

10 into slices to eat with .... friends.

Example	eats	eating	eat
1	because	if	but
2	and	to	or
3	made	makes	make
4	it	you	he
5	an	a	any
6	between	over	in
7	with	at	behind
8	one	two	some
9	took	take	taking
10	our	my	your

5 Look at the picture and read the story. Write some words to complete the sentences about the story. You can use 1, 2, 3, or 4 words.

The elephant

One day, Maria's teacher, Mrs. White, came to class with some great news. "The museum is having a competition! Every class is going to make an animal out of recycled materials," she said. Maria and the other children were excited.

The children brought materials from home. Soon, the class had 50 paper cups, 6 boxes of newspapers, 2 paper plates, and 2 plastic knives. "What kind of animal are we going to make with these things?" asked the children. Mrs. White smiled and said, "Think of different animals and how you can make them!"

The children made a large space in the center of the room and began to work. First, they made five very long things out of paper cups. Next, they made a large ball and a small ball out of newspaper.

Finally, they made the animal. The four long legs and a long nose, called a trunk, were made of the paper cups. The head and body were made from painted newspapers. The two ears were made of paper plates. The two long teeth, called tusks, were made of plastic knives. It was a beautiful elephant!

Examples

Mrs. White is Maria's ......teacher...... .

Mrs. White had ......some great news...... for Maria and her classmates.

Questions

1 There was a competition at the ....

2 Children had to make .... from recycled materials for the competition.

3 The children felt .... about the competition.

4 The children used all kinds of .... that they got from their homes.

5 They had .... of newspapers.

6 The elephant's legs were made of the ....

7 The children used .... to make the elephant's tusks.

6 Read the letter and write the missing words. Write one word on each line.

Example	......Dear...... Lucy,
1	Yesterday was my birthday .... my family and I went to a restaurant to have pizza.
2	I watched the cook make the pizza .... the kitchen.
3	First, she .... the dough out of flour and water.
4	Then she threw .... in the air to make it round.
	Next, she put tomatoes on the pizza.
	After that she added the cheese, mushrooms, and olives.
5	It .... delicious!
	Love,
	Mike

7 **Look at the three pictures. Write about this story. Write 20 or more words.**

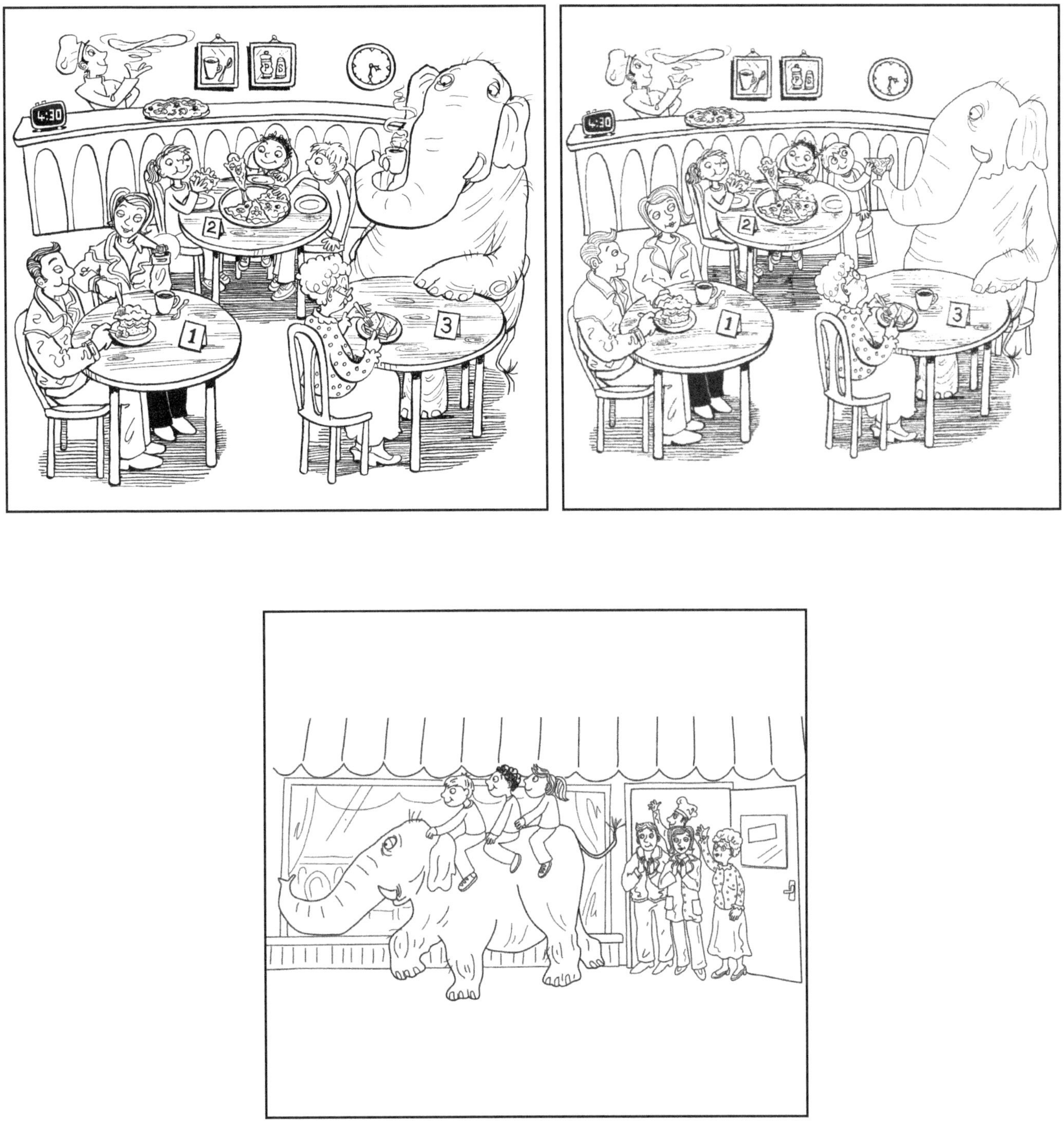

1

Teacher's card

Find the Differences

Student's card

Find the Differences

2

Teacher's card

John

What / making	?
What / made of	?
What / do first	?
How long / take to make	?
What / taste like	?

Katy

What / making	soup
What / made of	water, 3 carrots, and 4 onions
What / do first	cut the vegetables with a knife
How long / take to make	half an hour
What / taste like	very good

Find Information. Ask and answer.

Student's card

John

What / making	a sandwich
What / made of	bread, mayonnaise, and 3 tomatoes
What / do first	spread mayonnaise on the bread
How long / take to make	10 minutes
What / taste like	great

Katy

What / making	?
What / made of	?
What / do first	?
How long / take to make	?
What / taste like	?

Find Information. Ask and answer.

3 A birthday surprise

Daisy Betty

Tell the Story

Name: ....

Grade: ....

1 31 **Listen and draw lines. There is one example.**

2 32 Listen and write. There is one example.

Library Card

	Name:	David Richards
1	**Age:**	______
2	**School:**	______ Road School
3	**Favorite subject:**	______
4	**Number of books every month:**	______
5	**Topic of ezine project:**	Tree ______

3 33 What sports are the children good at?
Listen and write a letter in each box. There is one example.

Anna ☐

Nick [F]

John ☐

Katy ☐

Michael ☐

Lucy ☐

A

B

C

D

E

F

G

H

4 Listen and check (✓) the box. There is one example.

Which museum did Sarah go to?

A ☐

B ✓

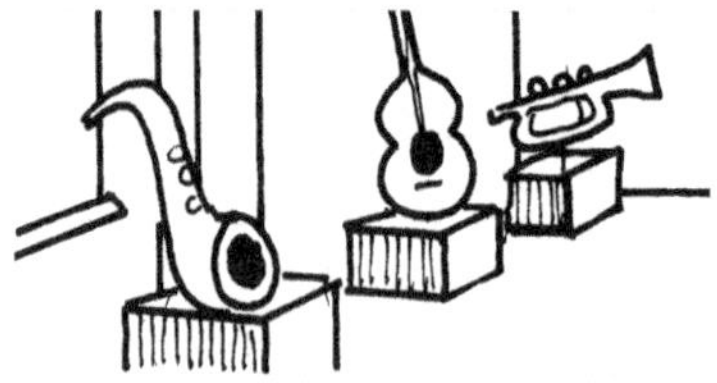

C ☐

1 How did Sarah travel to the museum?

A ☐

B ☐

C ☐

2 How long did it take to get to the museum?

30 MINUTES

A ☐

1 HOUR

B ☐

1 HOUR 30 MINUTES

C ☐

3 What did Sarah see at the museum?

A ☐

B ☐

C ☐

4 Why did Sarah fall?

A ☐

B ☐

C ☐

5 What did the museum send to Sarah?

A ☐

B ☐

C ☐

5 35 **Listen and color and write. There is one example.**

Test Units 7–8

Reading and Writing

Name: ....

Grade: ....

1 Look and read. Choose the correct words and write them on the lines. There is one example.

picnics — striped — extinct

engines — endangered species — butterflies — spring — bottles — spots

track and field — garbage — summer — ~~skiing~~ — eagles — sledding

This is a sport that you play in the winter. You stand up and go downhill in the snow. ......skiing......

1 Some creatures have these on their bodies. They are round. ....

2 When the weather is nice, people have these. They eat them outside, in a park or a field. ....

3 This is what you put in a can. You shouldn't leave it on the ground or throw it in lakes. ....

4 Many people like this sport. They play it in winter. They sit or lie down to do it. ....

5 You should recycle these when you have finished drinking from them. ....

6 They fly with four wings. They can be purple, red, or other colors. They are insects. ....

7 They are disappearing very quickly but there is still time to help them. They can be birds, animals, or insects. ....

8 We often play outside in this season because it's warm and sunny. It's before fall. ....

9 Some animals and insects have lines on them. Tigers and zebras are like this. ....

10 We usually play these sports outside. They can be running, jumping, or throwing. ....

2 Kim is asking Mr. Green some questions about the environment. What does Mr. Green say?

Read the conversation and choose the best answer.
Write a letter (A–H) for each answer.
You do not need to use all the letters.

Example

Kim: Excuse me, Mr. Green. Can I ask you some questions about the environment? It's for my ezine project.

Mr. Green: ...C...

Questions

1

Kim: When did you become interested in the environment?

Mr. Green: ....

2

Kim: Have you ever written a book about the environment?

Mr. Green: ....

3

Kim: What can we do to save trees?

Mr. Green: ....

4

Kim: How many endangered species are there today?

Mr. Green: ....

5

Kim: Thank you very much, Mr. Green.

Mr. Green: ....

A Yes. I've written two books about recycling.

B Yes, it is. I've won a prize.

C Of course. How can I help you? (***Example***)

D You're welcome, Kim. Good luck!

E You shouldn't throw paper away. Recycle it!

F You should build bird houses and plant flowers.

G I've wanted to learn about it since I was a young boy.

H A lot. And every year there are more.

3 Read the story. Choose a word from the box. Write the correct word next to numbers 1–5. There is one example.

example					
~~left~~	hurting	used	sunblock	walk	forgot
wanted	wear	yellow	sing		

Yesterday Peter, Mary, and John went walking in the hills. Before they left the house their mother said, "Peter, you should put a hat on." "Yes, Mom," he replied. "John, you should (**1**) .... sneakers." "Yes, Mom," he replied. "Mary, don't forget to put on your (**2**) .... if it gets hot." "Yes, Mom," Mary replied. But Peter hates hats, so he didn't take one. John doesn't like sneakers, so he wore plastic shoes, and Mary (**3**) .... to take the sunblock.

At noon they reached the top of a hill. The sun was very hot and Mary's arms were red. "I feel sick," said Peter.

"I feel sick, too," said Mary. John's foot was (**4**) .... But there was nowhere to hide from the sun. When they got home, they went to bed. The next day Peter was sick and couldn't play in his soccer game, Mary's arms were red and burned, and John couldn't (**5**) .... on his bad foot. "You should listen to me," said Mom.

"Yes, Mom," they replied.

(6) **Now choose the best name for the story. Check (✓) one box.**

A sunny day ☐ Listen to your mother ☐ Feeling sick ☐

4 Read the text. Choose the right words and write them on the lines.

Endangered animals

Example Every day more and ____more____ animals are becoming extinct.

1 In some countries people are ________ endangered animals.

2 ________ example, national parks take care of tigers in Russia.

3 They understand that there are people ________ want their fur.

4 Frogs are in danger all over ________ world. To make us think

5 ________ frogs more, people named 2008 "Year of the Frog."

6 Every year millions of Purple Spotted Butterflies ________

7 because they fly ________ roads and cars hit them.

8 In 2007 ________ Taiwan, they started to close the busy roads and now the butterflies are protected. There are still more

9 ________ 1,000 endangered insects and animals, but people

10 ________ helping to save them!

Example	more	many	most
1	protects	protected	protecting
2	For	By	At
3	we	who	what
4	a	one	the
5	with	about	over
6	died	dies	die
7	close to	out	straight
8	from	to	in
9	of	than	as
10	aren't	is	are

5 Look at the picture and read the story. Write some words to complete the sentences about the story. You can use 1, 2, 3, or 4 words.

Alex and the bull

Last summer Mr. and Mrs. Short took their two sons, Jack and Alex, to the country for a picnic. It was a nice sunny day.

The family found a large field and sat down on the grass. They put their picnic on a big red blanket on the grass. They were hungry, so they ate their sandwiches quickly. Then they had some cookies and drank some orange juice.

When Dad was putting their garbage into the can, he heard a loud noise. "Be careful!" he shouted. "It's a bull." The bull was very angry and it was coming after them.

The family didn't know what to do. Jack, the older boy, climbed up a tree. Dad hid behind the garbage can. Mom ran across the field. But where was little Alex? They couldn't see him. But Alex was hiding under the red blanket. And now the angry bull was close to him.

Suddenly Alex moved a little. The bull couldn't see Alex's head, his arms, or legs. He only saw that the red blanket was moving. The bull was really scared and ran away. Everyone was safe.

"Good job, Alex!" said Dad. "You saved us. Did you know that bulls don't like the color red?" Alex didn't know. But he knows now!

Examples

The Short family had ....a picnic.......... in the countryside.

The weather was ....sunny.......... .

Questions

1 They put the red blanket on ....

2 The family ate quickly because they were ....

3 Dad heard .... when he was putting garbage in the can.

4 Jack climbed up ....

5 Mom ran to the other side of the ....

6 They couldn't .... Alex.

7 The bull ran away because bulls don't like ....

6 Read the letter and write the missing words. Write one word on each line.

	Dear James,
Example	I'm ......having...... a wonderful vacation.
1	Yesterday I .... snowboarding and sledding with my
2	sister. And guess what! I've learned to ski! Have you ....
	been skiing? Yesterday I went downhill. I'm not very good
3	.... skiing, but I love it.
4	My sister is really good! .... Sunday she was in a race
	and she won a medal!
	In the evening we went to a restaurant to celebrate.
5	Do you .... skiing?
	Love,
	Ben

7 **Look at the three pictures. Write about this story. Write 20 or more words.**

1

Teacher's card

Find the Differences

Student's card

Find the Differences

2

Teacher's card

Tom

What sport / play	?
How often / practice	?
What / won	?
How old / when started playing	?
Been skiing	?

Sarah

What sport / play	badminton
How often / practice	2 nights a week
What / won	a silver medal
How old / when started playing	7
Been skiing	yes

Find Information. Ask and answer.

Student's card

Tom

What sport / play	tennis
How often / practice	3 days a week
What / won	a gold medal
How old / when started playing	8
Been skiing	no

Sarah

What sport / play	?
How often / practice	?
What / won	?
How old / when started playing	?
Been skiing	?

Find Information. Ask and answer.

3 Robert goes cycling

Tell the Story

Test key and audioscript

Scores are not shown on the tests themselves, giving you the flexibility to score in a way that suits your teaching situation. However, a scheme is given below that you may wish to use. Note that all four skills carry equal weight in the *Cambridge English: Young Learners* Tests. There are four complete tests in this section.

Marking Key

( ) = Acceptable extra words are placed in parentheses
/ = A single slash is placed between acceptable alternative words within an answer
// = A double slash is placed between acceptable alternative complete answers

Listening Key: F = adult female, M = adult male, FCH = female child, MCH = male child.

Test Units Welcome–2 pp. 76–90

Listening Part 1 (5 marks): page 76

Key: Lines should be drawn as follows:
1 Betty and girl writing at the desk, wearing a jacket
2 Harry and boy wearing pilot's uniform, carrying a plane
3 Sarah and shorter nurse, wearing glasses
4 Emma and girl dressed as firefighter, carrying hat, no shoes
5 Richard and boy on floor looking at plants

Track 16

Part One. Look at the picture. Listen and look. There is one example.

F: Hello, Mr. Green.
M: Hello, Mrs. Smith. Why are all the children in uniform?
F: They're wearing clothes for the jobs they're going to do.
M: I see. Where's my son, David?
F: He's there look. He's sitting on the floor. He's a mechanic.
M: Oh, yes. What's he doing?
F: He's working on a toy car.

Can you see the line? This is an example. Now you listen and draw lines.

M: Who are the other children here?
F: Can you see the girl with blond hair?
M: Is she writing in a notebook?
F: That's right. And she's wearing a jacket. That's Betty.
M: Does she want to be a reporter?
F: Yes. She's very good at English.
F: And can you see that boy in a hat? His name's Harry.
M: Is he carrying a plane under his arm?
F: Yes. His dad's a pilot and he wants to be one, too.
M: And who's the girl who's talking to my son?
F: The tall girl with blond hair?
M: No. I mean the short girl. She's dressed as a nurse, too, but she's wearing glasses.
F: Oh, yes. I see her. That's Sarah. She and your son have math together.
M: Is a girl named Emma here today?
F: Yes, she's a firefighter. Can you see her hat?
M: Is she wearing it?
F: No, it's really heavy. She's carrying it in her hand.
M: Why doesn't she have any shoes on?
F: She stood in some water and they're wet.
M: I think I know that boy with the bowl. He lives on our street.
F: The other boy on the floor?
M: Yes. Is his name Richard?
F: Yes. He's a very good soccer player.
M: But he's not dressed as one today.
F: That's right. He loves working with plants and animals. He wants to be a scientist.

Listening Part 2 (5 marks): page 77

Key: 1 13, 2 School, 3 White, 4 Saturday, 5 3.15//a quarter after three.

Track 17

Part Two. Listen and look. There is one example.

F: Hello. Thank you for calling. Can I have your name, please?
MCH: Yes. It's Peter Clark.
F: Clark. Is that C-L-A-R-K?
MCH: Yes. I'd like to be an actor in your new TV series.

Can you see the answer? Now you listen and write.

F: And how old are you Peter?
MCH: I'm 13. It was my birthday last week.
F: Did you have a nice birthday?
MCH: Yes, thank you.
F: Now what kind of things do you watch on TV, Peter?
MCH: Well, I like documentaries. There's a really good one called *Animal World* and I often watch cartoons, too. But my favorite is your TV series *School is Cool*.
F: OK, I got that. And who's your favorite movie actor?
MCH: Well, there are a lot of great movie and TV actors. But I think the best actor in the world is Will Black. I'm sorry, I mean Will *White*! His movies are great.
F: Well, Peter. We'd like you to do some acting for us. When can you come to Channel 3?
MCH: Is it possible to come on Sunday?
F: I'm sorry. More than 20 children are going to come on that day.
MCH: Oh, I see. Is Saturday OK then?
F: Yes, that's fine.
MCH: What time should I come? My mom says any time is OK.
F: Can I put your name down for a quarter after three?
MCH: Yes, thank you.
F: OK, Peter. We'll see you on the weekend.
MCH: Thank you very much. Goodbye.

Listening Part 3 (5 marks): page 78

Key: 1 B Mary and history, 2 G Katy and English, 3 D Emma and music, 4 C Bill and science, 5 F Tom and art.

Track 18

Part Three. Listen and look. There is one example. What is each student's favorite school subject?

F: Daisy. Tell me about your classmates. What are their favorite school subjects?
FCH: Let me see. Ben likes P.E. best. He plays badminton every Wednesday and he plays soccer every day. He says he's going to be a soccer player one day.

Can you see the letter E next to Ben? Now you listen and write a letter in each box.

F: Does anyone in your class like history?
FCH: Only one person.
F: Who's that?
FCH: Mary! She says that the teacher's really nice and she likes learning about the past. But the other people in my class think it's better to learn about living now.

F: What about your friend, Katy? What does she like?
FCH: Well, she wants to go to different countries.
F: Oh. So does she like geography?
FCH: She thinks it's OK. But she loves speaking to people from other countries, so she likes languages best. She has a big English dictionary. That's her favorite language.
F: What about Emma? She has a new computer, doesn't she? Does she like computer science?
FCH: She thinks the classes are very difficult and there's a lot of homework. She prefers music. She loves playing the guitar.
F: What other subjects do you study?
FCH: Well, a lot of people like science and it's Bill's favorite subject. He loves learning about animals. But he doesn't understand when the teacher talks about plants.
F: And what about art? Does anyone like those classes?
FCH: Oh, yes! A lot of people like them. Tom really likes painting and drawing. He's good at taking photographs, too.
F: Well, that's good. Your school sounds very nice.

Listening Part 4 (5 marks): page 79

Key: 1 B, 2 C, 3 B, 4 A, 5 A.
Note: Flyers test, Listening: This track has been recorded in British English so that students are exposed to both British and American English language and accent.

Track 19 *British English*

Part Four. Listen and look. There is one example. Where's Ben's mum going to work?
FCH: Hi Ben. How are you?
MCH: I'm really excited. My mum's going to start a new job!
FCH: Where's she going to work?
MCH: Well, she wanted to work in a TV studio but now she's got a job in the School of Archaeology at the university.
FCH: My dad works there, in the School of Art.

Can you see the check? Now you listen and check the box.
1 *What job is Ben's mum going to do?*
FCH: Is your mum going to be a scientist and study bones?
MCH: No, she's going to draw pictures of them.
FCH: Really? That's cool. But don't they do that on computers?
MCH: Sometimes. But Mum does it with a pencil.

2 *Who's Bens mum going to work for?*
MCH: Mum's going to work for a famous archaeologist!
FCH: Really? Is she going to work for Diggory Bones?
MCH: No, she's going to work for his brother, Archie Bones.
FCH: He isn't famous.
MCH: Yes, he is. He's more famous than Diggory Bones! And he's more famous than Doug Bones too.

3 *When's Ben's mum going to start her new job?*
FCH: When is your mum going to start her new job?
MCH: Well, she wanted to start on 1 July, but she can't.
FCH: Why not?
MCH: Because she has to work in her old job then.
FCH: Oh.
MCH: Yeah, but it's really exciting because she can start on 15 July and then on 21 July the School of Archaeology is going to be in a TV programme!

4 *What kind of TV programme is the School of Archaeology going to be in?*
FCH: Wow! Is the programme a documentary?
MCH: No. I asked her that. And it's not a quiz.
FCH: Oh. What is it then?
MCH: It's part of a sports programme. They want to show people that running and jumping can give you strong bones.

5 *What's Ben's mum's job now?*
FCH: Your mum's a dentist now, isn't she?
MCH: No, that's my dad. My mum's a history teacher.
FCH: Oh, right. Well, She's going to be on TV, so perhaps she's going to be a famous actress now.

Listening Part 5 (5 marks): page 80

Key: 1 green chair by the board, 2 blue English dictionary on the big desk, 3 yellow paper on the left of the wall, 4 PROJECT written on poster next to bookcase, 5 "Friday" on board.

Track 20

Part Five. Listen and look at the picture. There is one example.
M: Can you help me with this picture of a classroom?
FCH: Alright. What should I do?
M: Can you see the door?
FCH: Yes, I can.
M: OK. Well, color it black.
FCH: Right. I'm doing that now.

Can you see the black door? This is an example. Now you listen and color and write.
1
M: How many chairs can you see?
FCH: I can see six.
M: That's right. Can you see the one next to the board?
FCH: Yes. I think it's for the teacher. Should I color it?
M: What color do you think she'd like?
FCH: Green, I think.
M: Good idea. Do it that color.
2
M: Now look at the teacher's table. What can you see there?
FCH: There's a pen, an eraser, and a notebook.
M: And can you see the dictionaries?
FCH: Yes, I can. There are two.
M: That's right. Can you color the English dictionary?
FCH: What color?
M: Color it blue.
FCH: OK.
3
M: What can you see between the door and the bookcase?
FCH: There are two pieces of paper on the wall.
M: Good. Now color one of them.
FCH: Which one?
M: The one that's on the left.
FCH: OK. I'm going to do it yellow.
4
M: Can you write something now?
FCH: Yes, OK!
M: Can you write on the poster next to the bookcase?
FCH: Yes. What should I write?
M: Write the word PROJECT on it. You're going to do one in class soon!
FCH: Yes, we are. OK, I've written that now.
M: Good job.
5
M: What else do we need in the picture?
FCH: In my classroom, the teacher usually writes the day of the week on the board.
M: OK. Let's write that. What day is it today?
FCH: It's Friday.
M: Write that on the board.
FCH: Great! Soon it will be the weekend!

Reading & Writing Part 1 (10 marks): page 81

Key: 1 a dictionary, 2 cartoons, 3 a firefighter, 4 science, 5 pilots, 6 history, 7 geography, 8 dentists, 9 the news, 10 an ezine.

Reading & Writing Part 2 (5 marks): page 82

Key: 1 G, 2 B, 3 F, 4 A, 5 D.

Reading & Writing Part 3 (6 marks): page 83

Key: 1 newspaper, 2 forty//40, 3 quickly, 4 call, 5 important, 6 A fire in the park.

Reading & Writing Part 4 (10 marks): page 84

Key: 1 Do, 2 When, 3 there, 4 using, 5 every, 6 on, 7 should, 8 called, 9 wins, 10 Why.

Reading & Writing Part 5 (7 marks): page 85

Key: 1 Monday and Friday, 2 a great singer, 3 September, 4 six//6 5 school, 6 well, 7 second prize.

Reading & Writing Part 6 (5 marks): page 86

Key: 1 see//watch//catch, 2 asked, 3 had, 4 an, 5 of.

Reading & Writing Part 7 (15 marks): page 87

Key: Students' own answers

Speaking: pages 88–90

- Part 1. See general notes (page 6) in the Introduction for how to set up this part of the Speaking test. Give an example. Aim to elicit six differences from the student.
- Part 2. See general notes. Start by introducing Nick. *This is Nick. I don't know anything about him, but you do. So I'm going to ask you some questions. How old is Nick?* Ask students to answer the questions about Nick, then say *Now you ask me questions about Jenny* and point to the prompts on the Student's card.
- Part 3. See general notes. Start the story *It's Tuesday. There's going to be a science test on Friday. Michael wants to get 20 out of 20.*
- Part 4. Follow on the theme of what the student does in the evening by asking questions, such as: *What do you do in the evenings? Do you play sports? What time do you go to bed? Where do you do your homework? Tell me about your Saturday evenings.*, etc.

Test Units 3–4 pp. 91–105

Listening Part 1 (5 marks): page 91

Key: Lines should be drawn as follows:

1 Robert and boy on bridge, looking at cap in river
2 Michael and boy with long hair carrying a guitar
3 Helen and girl with short hair, in jacket and jeans, going into the movie theater
4 Jack and boy on bench with notebook in hand
5 Bill and boy outside café, sitting with his dad, paying the waiter

Track 21

Part One. Look at the picture. Listen and look. There is one example.

FCH: Thanks for bringing me out tonight, Dad. It's really exciting. A lot of my friends are going to the theater.
M: That's good.
FCH: Oh, look! There's my friend Anna!
M: The girl in the black shirt?
FCH: Yes. She's walking across the street to the theater.

Can you see the line? This is an example. Now you listen and draw lines.

M: What about Robert? Is he here yet?
FCH: I don't think so. He's always late!
M: Wait! That's him, over there!
FCH: Where?
M: He's on the bridge. Can you see him? He's looking at something in the river.
FCH: Oh, yes. Look. His hat's fallen into the water.
M: Oh, dear.
M: And who's that boy?
FCH: Do you mean the boy who's carrying a guitar?
M: Yes.
FCH: That's Michael. He's going to play in the theater. He's very good at music.
M: But look at his hair! It's very long!
FCH: A lot of boys have long hair these days, Dad.
FCH: Look! There's Helen. She's going into the theater.
M: Do you mean the girl who's wearing a dress?
FCH: No, she's wearing jeans and a jacket.
M: She has short hair. Do all your girl friends have short hair and the boys have long hair?
FCH: No, Dad!
M: Can you see any other friends?
FCH: Yes. There's one boy from my class sitting in the street.
M: Oh, yes. That's Jack, isn't it?
FCH: That's right.
M: Why does he have a notebook in his hand?
FCH: He's probably going to draw pictures!
M: In the street?
FCH: Yes. He *loves* art! He draws everything.
M: Where's your friend Bill? Is he coming to the theater?
FCH: He's in that café.
M: Is he sitting with his mom?
FCH: No. He's with his dad. And he's giving money to the waiter.

Listening Part 2 (5 marks): page 92

Key: 1 11//eleven, 2 Clock, 3 (her) aunt, 4 Saturday, 5 Walkers.

Track 22

Part Two. Listen and look. There is one example.

F: Excuse me. Can I ask you about your visit to London?
FCH: Yes, of course. What do you want to know?
F: What's your name, please?
FCH: It's Sarah Perez.
F: Perez. Is that P-E-R-E-Z?
FCH: Yes, that's right.

Can you see the answer? Now you listen and write.

F: Why are you in London, Sarah?
FCH: It's my birthday! We're going to go to London Zoo this morning.
F: Happy birthday! How old are you?
FCH: I'm 11 today.
F: That's great!
F: Where are you staying, Sarah? In a hotel?
FCH: Yes, we are.
F: And what's the name of the hotel?
FCH: It's called The Clock Hotel.
F: Oh, I know that. It's one of the oldest hotels in London.
F: And who are you in London with?
FCH: I'm here with my aunt.
F: Oh, so that woman's not your mom.
FCH: No, she couldn't come to London.
F: Why's that?
FCH: She's working. She can't take a vacation this month.
F: Now, how many days are you staying in London, Sarah?
FCH: We're here for six days.
F: When did you arrive?
FCH: Yesterday.

F: That's Monday. So you're going home on Saturday?
FCH: Yes. That's right.
F: And where are you going this afternoon?
FCH: To a toy store. I'm going to buy a birthday present.
F: That's nice. What's the name of the store?
FCH: Walkers.
F: I don't know that store. Please can you spell it for me?
FCH: Yes. It's W-A-L-K-E-R-S. Walkers.
F: Thanks. Well, I hope you enjoy your time here in London.
FCH: Thank you.

Listening Part 3 (5 marks): page 93

Key: 1 B William and leaves on fire, 2 E David and boy looking for watch in coat pocket, 3 G Mary and broken tooth, 4 H Jane and hurt leg, 5 D Alex and cut finger.

Track 23

Part Three. Listen and look. There is one example. What happened to the students in Robert's class?

M: Hello, Robert. Did you have a good day in school today?
MCH: Yes, it was fun. We learned about disasters in history.
M: The children in your class have a lot of disasters, don't they?
MCH: Yes. Do you remember what happened to Vicky last year?
M: Yes. That was a terrible accident. She was sailing with her dad when some lightning hit the boat. They jumped in the water and a helicopter came to get them.

Can you see the letter F next to Vicky? Now you listen and write a letter in each box.

M: And another friend had an accident last November, didn't he?
MCH: Oh, yes. William and his friends were jumping in some leaves in the backyard. His dad was burning things and the leaves caught fire. The boys had to go to the hospital. But they were OK.
M: That was lucky.
MCH: But one of the boys wasn't lucky.
M: Why?
MCH: Well, when they were jumping in the leaves, David put his watch in his coat pocket. He thought about it the next day, but it wasn't there. So he lost it.
M: Oh, dear.
MCH: And then there was Mary.
M: What happened to her?
MCH: She was going downstairs. Her little brother's toy car was there. She put her foot on it and she fell.
M: Did she break her arm?
MCH: No, she broke her tooth. She couldn't smile!
MCH: And her sister Jane fell down the next day, too.
M: Really?
MCH: Yes. She was climbing up a tree and it was really wet. She fell on the ground and she hurt her leg. She couldn't play soccer or volleyball for four weeks.
M: And did your friend Alex have an accident, too?
MCH: Oh, yes. He wanted to make a sandwich for lunch. He was cutting the bread with a big knife and he cut his finger.
M: Right. Well, I'm going to make some sandwiches for us now. But don't worry. I'll be careful!
MCH: That's good, Dad!

Listening Part 4 (5 marks): page 94

Key: 1 C, 2 B, 3 B, 4 A, 5 C.

Track 24

Part Four. Listen and look. There is one example. Where in town was the fire?

M: Did you hear about the fire in town yesterday?
F: Was it in the clothes store like last year?
M: No, it was in a café. But nobody was hurt. The firefighters came from the fire station very quickly.
F: That's good.

Can you see the check mark? Now you listen and check the box.

1 *Where was the café?*
F: Which café was it?
M: You know if you go from the train station straight up the High Street?
F: Yes?
M: Well, it's on the first street on the left.
F: Oh, yes. I know. That's Mr. Green's café. But it's not my favorite. I like the one that's on the first street on the right. I go there with my friend on Friday mornings.

2 *Where did the fire start?*
F: And where did the fire start? Was it in the kitchen?
M: No, it was because of the storm yesterday evening. The lightning hit the building.
F: That happened to me last year and my computer caught fire.
M: Well, this fire started because the lightning hit the clock on the wall outside.
F: Wow! That's a surprise.

3 *What was Mr. Green doing when the fire started?*
F: Was Mr. Green in the café when the fire started?
M: Yes, he was. He was talking.
F: On the phone? That's dangerous when there's a storm.
M: He was talking to one of his customers, Mrs. Smith. She goes shopping and then goes to the café for a cup of coffee.

4 *What did the customers do when the fire started?*
F: Did the customers run out into the street?
M: You shouldn't run when there's a fire. No, they were very good. They all walked out of the café and went home.
F: Didn't anyone stand in the street and watch?
M: It was raining a lot so I don't think they wanted to do that.

5 *Where did the man hear about the fire?*
F: How do you know about the fire? There wasn't anything on TV last night.
M: I know. My friend told me about it.
F: Well, maybe it's going to be on the radio news today.

Listening Part 5 (5 marks): page 95

Key: 1 a green castle door next to the police officer, 2 a red small coffee cup, 3 PIZZA written on the board outside the café, 4 blue T-shirt on boy listening to music, 5 AUGUST is written on the sign above "Park."

Track 25

Part Five. Listen and look at the picture. There is one example.

M: Can you help me with this picture? Can you see the castle?
FCH: Yes. It looks very strong.
M: Yes, it does. Can you color it gray?
FCH: OK. That's a good color for a castle.

Can you see the gray castle? This is an example. Now you listen and color and write.

1
M: Now can you color the castle door?
FCH: Which one do you mean?
M: The one where the police officer is standing.
FCH: Oh, OK.
M: Why don't you color it green?
FCH: Right. I'm doing that now.

2
M: Now look at the café. Can you see the two women sitting outside? They're both drinking coffee.
FCH: Yes, I can see them.
M: Why don't you color one of their coffee cups?
FCH: OK. Should I color the one next to the piece of cake?
M: No. Color the other one.
FCH: Right. I think I'll color it red.
M: That's a good idea.
3
M: I think you can have something to eat here, too. Look, the cook's going to write something on the board outside.
FCH: Oh, yes. What do you think he's going to write?
M: I think it's PIZZA. Do you want to write it for him?
FCH: OK.
4
M: Can you see those boys? You could color one of their T-shirts.
FCH: OK. I'm going to color the T-shirt of the boy listening to music.
M: What color are you going to do it?
FCH: I'm going to do it blue.
5
FCH: It looks nice where the boys are, doesn't it?
M: Yes, it does. Why don't you write the name? It's called August Park.
FCH: Oh, like the month?
M: Exactly.
FCH: OK. I'm writing that now.
M: Excellent. What a great picture!

Reading & Writing Part 1 (10 marks): page 96

Key: 1 a bridge, 2 a castle, 3 October, 4 fire stations, 5 December, 6 museums, 7 July, 8 an airport, 9 a movie theater, 10 February.

Reading & Writing Part 2 (5 marks): page 97

Key: 1 H, 2 D, 3 A, 4 F, 5 G.

Reading & Writing Part 3 (6 marks): page 98

Key: 1 paintings, 2 across, 3 most, 4 minutes, 5 fall, 6 An exciting story.

Reading & Writing Part 4 (10 marks): page 99

Key: 1 this, 2 sailing, 3 on, 4 there, 5 or, 6 came, 7 into, 8 waited, 9 her, 10 worst.

Reading & Writing Part 5 (7 marks): page 100

Key: 1 three/3 friends, 2 half an hour//30 minutes, 3 11.00// eleven/11 o'clock, 4 fell in(to), 5 swim (very well), 6 terrible, 7 June.

Reading & Writing Part 6 (5 marks): page 101

Key: 1 on, 2 had, 3 second // 2nd, 4 to, 5 tell.

Reading & Writing Part 7 (15 marks): page 102

Key: Students' own answers

Speaking: pages 103–105

- Part 1. See general notes (page 6) in the Introduction for how to set up this part of the Speaking test. Give an example. Aim to elicit six differences from the student.
- Part 2. See general notes. Introduce Mary. Say *This is Mary. She went out this morning. I don't know anything about her, but you do. I'm going to ask you some questions. Where did Mary go this morning?* Ask the student to answer all the questions about Mary then say, *Now you ask me questions about Richard.* Point to the prompts on the Student's card.
- Part 3. See general notes. Start the story *Yesterday, Fred was out in the park with his dog.*
- Part 4. Follow on the theme of going out in the town by asking *How often do you go to town? Where do you go in town? Who do you go to town with? What do you usually do in town? Tell me about your favorite store/restaurant in town.,* etc.

Test Units 5–6 pp. 106–120

Listening Part 1 (5 marks): page 106

Key: Lines should be drawn as follows:
1 Fred and man sitting on chair, reading old newspapers
2 Lucy and girl next to food bin, drinking from a bottle
3 Sarah and woman in dress with box of plastic
4 Alex and man with wooden box, looking worried
5 Jim and boy with backpack on back, climbing onto metal bin

Track 26

Part One. Look at the picture. Listen and look. There is one example.
F: Thanks for coming to help, Tom.
MCH: There are a lot of people here today, aren't there?
F: Yes, and I know them all. … Right over there is the paper bin. We put newspapers, cardboard, and old paper in there.
MCH: Who's the woman who's standing by that bin?
F: That's Mary. She comes here every week.
MCH: But she's going to put metal in it! That's not right!
F: No. She's going to need some help.

Can you see the line? This is an example. Now you listen and draw lines.
MCH: Who's that man? He's sitting on the chair.
F: Oh, that's Fred. He comes every week, too.
MCH: What is he doing?
F: He's just reading the old newspapers. He doesn't put anything in the bins!
F: Now … the bin for old food is on the right.
MCH: Who's the girl next to it?
F: The one eating an apple?
MCH: No, she's drinking something from a glass bottle.
F: Oh. That's Lucy.
MCH: I hope she's not going to put her bottle in that bin!
F: People are putting a lot of things into the plastic bin today. Look at Sarah.
MCH: But she only has one plastic bag.
F: No, not her, the other woman. She's wearing a dress. Look at the box by her feet.
MCH: Wow! She has a lot of plastic!
F: Yes. Her family eats a lot of food!
MCH: Does that man know what to do?
F: Which one?
MCH: He's holding a wooden box.
F: Oh, that's Alex.
MCH: Is he OK? I think he's looking for something.
F: Yes. He recycles everything! And he puts it all in the right place, but I think he's lost his son.
MCH: What's his son's name?
F: It's Jim.
MCH: The boy with the backpack on his back?
F: Yes. Oh, dear! He's climbing on the metal recycling bin! Quick! Stop him!
MCH: OK. I'm going now. Hey!

Listening Part 2 (5 marks): page 107

Key: 1 school, 2 Children, 3 spiders, 4 120, 5 845 3790.

Track 27

Part Two. Listen and look. There is one example.

M: Hello. Are you Katy Barker?
FCH: Yes, I am.
M: I'm from the town newspaper. We'd like to write about your special birthday party next month. Can you spell your last name, Barker, for me please?
FCH: Yes, it's B-A-R-K-E-R.
M: Thank you.

Can you see the answer? Now you listen and write.

M: Tell me about your party.
FCH: It's going to be different from other parties.
M: Why?
FCH: Because we're going to sell food not eat it.
M: And where are you going to do that? At home?
FCH: In school. My teacher says it's OK.
M: And how did you get the idea?
FCH: Well, it started in my geography class.
M: Oh, yes?
FCH: Yes. We learned that a lot of people in the world are hungry. So we're going to sell food to get some money.
M: Who will you give the money to?
FCH: It's called "Help the Children." They give two meals a day to children who don't have very much food.
M: It's a great idea. What are you going to cook?
FCH: I'm going to make chocolate spiders. But other people are going to make cakes and cookies.
M: I'd like to buy some!
M: And how many people are going to be at the party?
FCH: There are about 30 children in my class, but people from other classes can come, too.
M: So it's for all the school?
FCH: Yes. I think about 120 people are going to be there.
M: Really? It's going to be great!
FCH: Yes.
M: What's your phone number? We can talk again after the party.
FCH: It's 845 3790.
M: Thank you and good luck, Katy!

Listening Part 3 (5 marks): page 108

Key: 1 G Katy and hand recording family singing, 2 B David and baby made of shapes, 3 H Richard and candy, 4 A Sally and picture of smelly cheese, 5 F John and bicycle.

Track 28

Part Three. Listen and look. There is one example. What did the children in the class make?

F: What are all these things in your classroom?
FCH: Oh, we're studying the senses. We had to make something about a sense.
F: So, what did you make, Anna?
FCH: I chose the sense of touch, so this is my project.
F: It looks like an animal.
FCH: Yes, it's a tiger. I made it with fur. It feels nice.

Can you see the letter D next to Anna? Now you listen and write a letter in each box.

F: Tell me about the other people in your class. Did anyone choose the sense of hearing?
FCH: Yes. This is Katy's project. She made a CD with sounds of people in her family. You can hear her mom, her dad, and her sisters. They're talking and singing. And you can hear her little baby sister, too. She sounds really angry!
F: Which is David's project?
FCH: His project's a picture about the sense of sight. He's using three shapes: circles, triangles, and squares.
F: Is his picture a house?
FCH: No, it's a baby with a hat on.
F: I think the hat looks like a roof, don't you?
FCH: Yes, it does.
F: What about taste? Who chose that?
FCH: Oh, that's Richard. Can you see? His project's a box with food in it. He made it all. There is some candy, some chocolate, and some cake. The candy tastes really nice!
F: Did Sally choose taste, too?
FCH: Why?
F: Well, there's a picture of some cheese with her name on it.
FCH: Oh, no! Her project's about smell. That cheese was really strong. It was horrible. It smelled like old socks! We had to open the classroom windows all morning.
F: And what's John's project?
FCH: He's really smart. He's making a bicycle. It's made of recycled metal and it can move! But it sounds strange when you move it. It sounds like an old car!

Listening Part 4 (5 marks): page 109

Key: 1 C, 2 A, 3 B, 4 A, 5 C.

Track 29

Part Four. Listen and look. There is one example. Where was Jason's birthday party?

F: How was your birthday, Jason?
MCH: Fine thanks, Grandma.
F: Did you spend the day at home?
MCH: No, we didn't.
F: Did you go to the movie theater?
MCH: No. We had a party at a restaurant.
F: That's nice.

Can you see the check mark? Now you listen and check the box.

1 *Why didn't Grandma go to the birthday party?*
F: I'm sorry I couldn't come to your party, Jason.
MCH: It's OK, Grandma. You were sick.
F: No. I wasn't sick. Your grandfather was sick.
MCH: Really? Is he all right now?
F: He's fine. He's working in the backyard today.

2 *What did Jason eat?*
F: What did you eat at the party?
MCH: Well, there were fries, salad, and pasta.
F: That's nice. What did you have?
MCH: I didn't have any pasta.
F: Why?
MCH: I wasn't very hungry. So I just ate some fries.
F: Did they taste nice?
MCH: They tasted OK. But they smelled horrible.

3 *What did the birthday cake look like?*
F: Did you have a birthday cake?
MCH: Well, yes, but there was a problem. Mom bought one from a store. It was very funny.
F: Why?
MCH: It had a doll who was dancing on the top!
F: Couldn't your mom find a cake that looked like a train or a soccer ball?
MCH: No. The store didn't have any others. But it tasted nice. And everyone sang "Happy Birthday."

4 *What was Jason's favorite present?*
F: What presents did you get?
MCH: My parents bought me a really nice book about science. And my friends bought me a toy spider.
F: That's nice. What was your favorite present?
MCH: Your present, Grandma!
F: Really? You like the watch?
MCH: I love it, thank you. Look. I'm wearing it now.

5 *When is Jason going to visit his grandparents?*
F: When can you come to see us, Jason? On Thursday?
MCH: Saturday's better. You see, I have an exam in school on Friday, so it's not a good idea to come before that.
F: Fine. Make sure you're hungry! I'm going to cook you a big meal and make you a cake, too.
MCH: Thank you!

Listening Part 5 (5 marks): page 110

Key: 1 COOK is written on the cat's hat, 2 four green pieces of pepper on the pizza, 3 large blue bowl on the right of the picture, 4 red round present, 5 HAPPY written above BIRTHDAY on the card.

Track 30

Part Five. Listen and look at the picture. There is one example.
FCH: Look at this picture!
M: Yes, it's Tom the cat's birthday.
FCH: He's cooked a pizza for his birthday meal.
M: That's right. But look. He's not a very good cook.
FCH: Why not?
M: The pizza crust is black. Do you want to color it?
FCH: OK.

Can you see the black pizza crust? This is an example. Now you listen and color and write.

1
M: Do you want to write something in the picture?
FCH: Yes! Can I write on Tom's hat?
M: Of course. Write COOK on it.
FCH: OK! That means someone who makes meals, doesn't it?
M: That's right.
FCH: OK. I've done that now.
M: Good!
2
FCH: What are those things on top of the pizza?
M: Do you mean the tomatoes?
FCH: No. The four things that are long and thin.
M: I think those are pieces of pepper.
FCH: Right. What color can we make them?
M: What about green?
FCH: OK. That's a good color.
3
M: Tom has salad to eat with his pizza. Can you see the bowl?
FCH: Which one? The small one on the left of the picture?
M: No, the big one on the right. Do you want to color it?
FCH: Yes, please.
M: OK. Let's make it a nice blue color.
FCH: Right. I'm doing that now.
4
M: Can you see Tom's presents?
FCH: Yes, he has a lot! He's a lucky cat!
M: Yes. Why don't you color one of the presents red?
FCH: Which one?
M: The round one, I think.
FCH: OK. That looks nice.
5
M: Tom has some birthday cards.
FCH: Yes. I think they're from his friends.
M: And he's writing one with his tail.
FCH: Oh, yes. What's he writing?
M: I think it says HAPPY BIRTHDAY. Can you finish writing it for him?
FCH: OK. What a nice birthday!

Reading & Writing Part 1 (10 marks): page 111

Key: 1 plates, 2 meals, 3 fur, 4 paper, 5 glass, 6 salt, 7 gold, 8 a knife, 9 a scarf, 10 spoons.

Reading & Writing Part 2 (5 marks): page 112

Key: 1 E, 2 G, 3 B, 4 D, 5 H.

Reading & Writing Part 3 (6 marks): page 113

Key: 1 taste, 2 look, 3 soft, 4 sound, 5 terrible, 6 A new person in the family.

Reading & Writing Part 4 (10 marks): page 114

Key: 1 because, 2 to, 3 make, 4 you, 5 an, 6 in, 7 with, 8 one, 9 take, 10 your.

Reading & Writing Part 5 (7 marks): page 115

Key: 1 museum, 2 an animal, 3 excited, 4 materials, 5 six/6 boxes, 6 paper cups, 7 plastic knives.

Reading & Writing Part 6 (5 marks): page 116

Key: 1 so//and, 2 in, 3 made//mixed, 4 it//the dough, 5 was//tasted.

Reading & Writing Part 7 (15 marks): page 117

Key: Students' own answers

Speaking: pages 118–120.

- Part 1. See general notes (page 6) in the introduction for how to set up this part of the Speaking test. Give an example. Aim to elicit six differences from the student.
- Part 2. See general notes. Start by introducing John. Say *This is John with his sister, Katy, in the kitchen. I don't know anything about John but you do. I'm going to ask you some questions. What is John making?* Ask the students to answer all the questions about John, then say *Now you ask me questions about Katy.* Point to the prompts on the Student's card.
- Part 3. See general notes. Start the story *It's January twentieth and it's Betty and Daisy's mom's birthday.*
- Part 4. Follow on the theme of birthdays by asking *What do you like doing on your birthday? Tell me about the best birthday you have had.*, etc.

Test Units 7–8 pp. 121–135

Listening Part 1 (5 marks): page 121

Key: Lines should be drawn as follows:
1 Betty and tall girl standing in striped team's goal
2 Daisy and girl looking at butterfly on her glove
3 Jane and girl with long hair in her eyes
4 Paul and boy with dog
5 William and boy fallen down on ice by piece of wood

Track 31

Part One. Look at the picture. Listen and look. There is one example.
M: I've never played ice hockey. It looks fun.
FCH: Yes. My friends love it. And Alex is the best.
M: Which boy is he?
FCH: He's in front of the goal in a striped sweater.
M: What's he doing?
FCH: He's hitting the puck (that's like the ball in ice hockey). I think he's going to get a point.

Can you see the line? This is an example. Now you listen and draw lines.
M: Is your friend Betty playing?

FCH: Yes. She's on the striped team, too. She's the very tall girl.
M: Is she in the other goal?
FCH: Yes, she is. She's the best goalie the striped team has ever had.
M: And who's that girl? She isn't playing!
FCH: The girl who's pulling her sock up?
M: No, the one who's looking at her glove.
FCH: Oh. That's Daisy.
M: What's she doing?
FCH: She's looking at a butterfly! She's always dreaming.
M: Is your friend Jane here?
FCH: Yes, she is. But I don't think she's playing very well.
M: How do you know?
FCH: Because she has really long hair and it's dropping in her eyes! She can't see.
M: Does she wear glasses sometimes?
FCH: Yes, but she's not wearing them now. She doesn't wear them when she's playing ice hockey.
M: Good idea. It's very dangerous.
M: Ha ha! Look! There's a dog on the ice!
FCH: Oh, no! Where did it come from?
M: I don't know, but that boy is having problems with it!
FCH: Oh, that's Paul. I think he's trying to take it back to his dad, but he's not very good at skating.
FCH: Oh, no! William's fallen over!
M: Where?
FCH: He's there on the left. I think there's some garbage on the ice. Is it a piece of wood?
M: Oh, yes. Do you think he's going to be OK?
FCH: I hope so! He's the best player on that team!

Listening Part 2 (5 marks): page 122

Key: 1 twelve//12, 2 Charter, 3 science, 4 five//5, 5 frogs.

Track 32

Part Two. Listen and look. There is one example.

F: Welcome to the library.
MCH: Thank you.
F: Now, I'd like to ask you a few questions for your library card. Let's start with your name.
MCH: It's David Richards.
F: Can you spell Richards, please?
MCH: Yes, it's R-I-C-H-A-R-D-S.
F: Thank you.

Can you see the answer? Now you listen and write.

F: Now, David. I need to know your age.
MCH: OK. Now or next week? It's my birthday on Sunday.
F: I see. Let's write your age next week.
MCH: I'm going to be 12. I've just started a new school.
F: OK. And I need the name of your school, please.
MCH: OK. It's Charter Road School.
F: Can you spell it for me, please?
MCH: Yes, it's C-H-A-R-T-E-R. Charter.
F: Thanks.
F: And now we have to write your favorite school subject. You have a badminton racket in your bag, so I think you like P.E.
MCH: Well, I do. But it isn't my favorite. I've come to the library to borrow a lot of books about science. That's my favorite subject.
F: OK. And how many books do you want every month?
MCH: Well, on vacation, I read about eight books a month, but when I'm in school I don't have time for so many.
F: Mm. OK. Well, let's put five.
MCH: That sounds good.
F: Right. What kind of book do you want today?
MCH: Well, I'm doing a project for the school ezine. I want to write about the tree frogs in South America.
F: That's lucky. We got a new book about them this week.
MCH: Great.

Listening Part 3 (5 marks): page 123

Key: 1 D Katy and swimming, 2 H Anna and skiing, 3 C John and track and field, 4 A Lucy and basketball, 5 B Michael and climbing.

Track 33

Part Three. Listen and look. There is one example. What sports are the children good at?

M: Mrs. Sims, a lot of children in the school are good at sports. Should we give out some class sports prizes this year?
F: That sounds like a good idea, Mr. Jakes.
M: What sports do the children in your class enjoy?
F: Well, Nick loves sailing. Did you know he's been in a world competition with his father?
M: Wow! That's fantastic.

Can you see the letter F next to Nick? Now you listen and write a letter in each box.

M: And what about his sister, Katy? Is she good at a sport?
F: Yes. All her family are good at sports, but her favorite is swimming. She goes to the pool in town every morning before school. She's won four gold medals.
M: Really? That's wonderful.
M: Now what about Anna? She lived in Canada, is she good at snowboarding?
F: Yes, but her best sport is skiing. She can go downhill very fast. She always finishes first.
M: Who else is there? Oh, yes, John! What can he do?
F: He's *really* good at track and field. He's won six prizes at his club for the high jump. His mom says he jumps over things at home, too! He can't stop!
M: We have a volleyball team in the school. Is anyone in your class good at that? Lucy's good at playing ball games.
F: Yes. But she's good at basketball. She's the best player in my class. She's very good at scoring points and she can run fast.
M: Now what about Michael?
F: Well, he's terrible at most sports! But he's good at climbing. He's in a club and he often goes up mountains with his father on vacations.
M: Well, all the children in your class sound fantastic. Why don't we give them all a prize?
F: Great!

Listening Part 4 (5 marks): page 124

Key: 1 B, 2 C, 3 A, 4 B, 5 A.

Track 34

Part Four. Listen and look. There is one example.

Which museum did Sarah go to?

M: Hello, Sarah! How was your school trip to the museum? Did you see a lot of beautiful art?
FCH: We didn't go there, Grandpa.
M: Oh. Where did you go?
FCH: Well, I wanted to go to a museum and learn about music, but we went to the science museum.

Can you see the check mark? Now you listen and check the box.

1 *How did Sarah travel to the museum?*
M: How did you get there?
FCH: It's a long way. It's too far to walk. And my mom couldn't take me and my friends there in her car because she was busy. We went on the school bus.

2 *How long did it take to get to the museum?*
M: How long did it take?
FCH: It was really slow. It took one and a half hours!
M: Why?
FCH: Well, it only took half an hour to get from the school to the town. But there was a cycling competition close to the museum. There were a lot of people on bicycles! So the last part took *one* hour!

3 *What did Sarah see at the museum?*
M: So what did you see in the museum? The computer section? It's wonderful!
FCH: No. That was closed.
M: Oh, dear. So where did you go? To the dinosaurs?
FCH: Some people from my class went there, but my friends and I went to see the snakes.

4 *Why did Sarah fall?*
M: Did you have a nice time?
FCH: Not really. I had an accident.
M: Oh, no! What happened?
FCH: Well, I was walking through the museum when I fell over.
M: Are you sure no one pushed you?
FCH: No, there was some water on the floor. My friends thought I was playing. So they started to laugh at me.
M: Oh, dear!

5 *What did the museum send to Sarah?*
M: Did anyone from the museum say sorry?
FCH: Yes. They sent me a card the next day. It was beautiful! It had a picture of a bat on it.
M: That's good.
FCH: And they sent me two tickets to go again next month.
M: Are you going to go?
FCH: Yes. Would you like to come with me, Grandpa?
M: Yes, please!

Listening Part 5 (5 marks): page 125

Key: 1 a green fish on the grass, 2 a yellow bird in the sky, 3 PICNICS is written on the sign on the trunk of the tree, above "here," 4 PAPER written on the trash can on the tree, 5 a blue plastic bag with sunblock next to it.

Track 35

Part Five. Listen and look at the picture. There is one example.
F: The children are having a nice picnic in this picture.
MCH: Can I color it?
F: OK. What do you want to color first?
MCH: Can you see the cows in the field?
F: Yes.
MCH: I'm going to color the one that's sitting down.
F: What color are you going to do it?
MCH: I'm going to color it black.

Can you see the black cow? This is an example. Now you listen and color and write.

1
F: The two boys are fishing in the river.
MCH: Should I color one of the fish? That one's very beautiful.
F: Which one?
MCH: The one on the grass with a spotted tail.
F: OK. Color that one green.
MCH: Right.
2
MCH: I'm going to color a bird now.
F: Which one? The one in the tree?
MCH: No. The one that's flying. Look at its big wings.
F: What color are you going to do it?
MCH: Yellow, I think.
F: OK. That's a great color.
3
F: Do you want to write something now?
MCH: OK. What should I write?
F: Can you see the piece of paper on the tree?
MCH: Yes, I can. It's under the bird and above the trash can.
F: That's right. Can you write PICNICS on it?
MCH: Yes, OK. That's where people can do that.
F: Right!
4
MCH: There isn't any trash in the picture, is there?
F: No. Everyone has put it in the cans.
MCH: What do you think is in the one on the tree?
F: I think it's for paper. Why don't you write PAPER on it?
MCH: OK. Good idea.
5
MCH: The children have some plastic bags.
F: Yes. One of them has the food in it.
MCH: I'm going to color the other one, I think. It has some sunblock next to it.
F: OK. Color that bag blue.
MCH: Right. I've finished. This is a very good picture.

Reading & Writing Part 1 (10 marks): page 126

Key: 1 spots, 2 picnics, 3 garbage, 4 sledding, 5 bottles, 6 butterflies, 7 endangered species, 8 summer, 9 striped, 10 track and field.

Reading & Writing Part 2 (5 marks): page 127

Key: 1 G, 2 A, 3 E, 4 H, 5 D.

Reading & Writing Part 3 (6 marks): page 128

Key: 1 wear, 2 sunblock, 3 forgot, 4 hurting, 5 walk, 6 Listen to your mother.

Reading & Writing Part 4 (10 marks): page 129

Key: 1 protecting, 2 For, 3 who, 4 the, 5 about, 6 die, 7 close to, 8 in, 9 than, 10 are.

Reading & Writing Part 5 (7 marks): page 130

Key: 1 the grass, 2 hungry, 3 a (loud) noise//the/a bull, 4 a tree, 5 field, 6 see, 7 (the color) red.

Reading & Writing Part 6 (5 marks): page 131

Key: 1 went, 2 ever, 3 at, 4 On//Last, 5 like//love//enjoy.

Reading & Writing Part 7 (15 marks): page 132

Key: Students' own answers

Speaking: pages 133–135

- Part 1. See general notes (page 6) in the introduction for how to set up this part of the Speaking test. Give an example. Aim to elicit six differences from the student.
- Part 2. See general notes. Start by introducing Tom. Say *This is Tom. He's at the Sports Club party. I don't know anything about him, but you do. I'm going to ask you some questions. What sports does Tom play?* Get the students to answer all the questions about Tom, then say *Now you ask me questions about Sarah.* Point to the prompts on the Student's card.
- Part 3. See general notes. Start the story *It's Robert's birthday today and he's nine years old. He's very happy.*
- Part 4. Follow on the sports and seasons theme by asking *What sports do you play? What sports does your family watch on TV? Which season is your favorite? Where do you like to go in winter? Tell me what you like to do in summer.*, etc.